D1830335

CEYLON CURRENCY
BRITISH PERIOD
1796-1936

CEYLON CURRENCY
BRITISH PERIOD
1796-1936

B. W. FERNANDO

WITH A FOREWORD BY
H. W. CODRINGTON

GYAN

Published by

GYAN

Gyan Publishing House
5, Ansari Road
Daryaganj, New Delhi-110002
Phone: 011-47034999, 9811692060
E-mail: books@gyanbooks.com

Distribution Network
gyanbooks.com
India, USA, Canada, UK, Australia, France

© Publisher

All rights reserved. No part of this work may be reproduced, stored, adapted, or transmitted in any form or by any means, electronic, mechanical, photocopying, micro-filming, recording or otherwise, or translated in any language, without the prior written permission of the copyright owner and the publisher.

ISBN : 978-81-212-3213-5 (PB)
First Published, Colombo

2nd Impression 2020

Printed at: Gyan Press, Delhi.

The book is sold subject to the condition that it shall not, by way of trade or otherwise, be lent, resold, hired out, or otherwise circulated without the prior publisher's written consent.

Ceylon Currency
Author: B. W. Fernando

CEYLON CURRENCY

BRITISH PERIOD

1796-1936

BY

B. W. FERNANDO,

Principal Assistant Accountant,

General Treasury, Colombo.

With a FOREWORD

BY

H. W. CODRINGTON, Esq., B.A. (Oxon.), F.R.N.S.

Late of the Ceylon Civil Service,

AUTHOR OF

"Ceylon Coins and Currency",

"A Short History of Ceylon", &c.

PRINTED AT THE CEYLON GOVERNMENT PRESS, COLOMBO.

To be purchased at the GOVERNMENT RECORD OFFICE, COLOMBO; *price Rs. 2·50.*

1939

2——J. N. 81971–305 (2/39)

FOREWORD.

Mr. B. W. Fernando's work on the currency of Ceylon during the British Period, though perhaps not appealing to the general public, supplies a want and will be appreciated by those interested in the subject, based as it is on records official and unofficial. Mr. Fernando has divided his thesis into two main heads, namely, the coinage and the paper currency. Under the first he deals with the British copper and silver struck locally and in the United Kingdom, with the introduction of sterling, with the subsequent supremacy of the Indian rupee, and finally with the decimal subsidiary tokens with which we are now familiar. Under the second head we read of the Dutch Kredit Brieven and "cash notes", the early British rixdollar and sterling notes, the notes issued by the banks, and lastly the restoration of a Government currency.

Mr. Fernando is to be congratulated on his painstaking researches, for which the student will be duly grateful. His work is a credit to him and through him to the Public Service of Ceylon.

November 30, 1938. H. W. CODRINGTON.

PREFACE.

THE purpose of this book is to present in plain language a brief history of the coinage and paper currency of Ceylon since the British occupation. It consists of material collected from both official and unofficial publications and records, primarily for my own information. The notes were published in the shape of a series of articles in the " Ceylon Trade Journal " in its issues for the months April to August, 1938, with a view to creating an interest in currency matters in the public mind, in view of a proposal to change the currency system of the Island. A few additions and alterations have since been made, and the Orders in Council and Proclamations relating to the Coinage and the " Revised " Ordinance regulating the Paper Currency included as Appendices. Though printed at the Government Press and a greater part of it based on official records, this compilation is not issued as an " official " publication and I alone am responsible for the statements it contains. I have endeavoured to avoid errors as far as possible, and if any that are noticed are communicated to me it will be appreciated.

I owe a deep debt of gratitude to Mr. H. W. Codrington, late of the Ceylon Civil Service, for his FOREWORD, for some very helpful suggestions, and for important matter obtained from his scholarly work " Ceylon Coins and Currency ". I must also express my gratitude to Mr. C. H. Collins, Deputy Financial Secretary, Mr. S. Phillipson, Controller of Establishments, and to Mr. J. L. Stanislaus, Financial Assistant and Accountant, Treasury, for advice and encouragement.

My thanks are due to Mr. W. T. Loos, Office Assistant to the Chief Secretary, to Mr. N. U. Jayawardene, Commercial Assistant to the Director of Commerce and Industries, and to Messrs. C. S. Kreltszheim, H. M. de Mel and E. B. Wiratunga of the Treasury for assistance rendered in the production of this book.

I have also to express my obligation to the Printing Committee for kindly allowing this to be printed at the Government Press, to the Surveyor-General for supplying blocks for the illustrations, to the Director of the Colombo Museum and Mr. M. F. S. Goonatilaka for placing at my disposal coins and notes for the purpose, and to the Government Press for the neat get-up of this book.

The General Treasury,
Colombo, February 20, 1939.

B. W. FERNANDO.

CONTENTS.

PART I.—THE COINAGE.

PART II.—THE PAPER CURRENCY.

APPENDICES.

(i.) Law regulating the coinage and the paper currency.

(ii.) Statistics.

ILLUSTRATIONS.*

* Normal size of coins shown.

No. 1.

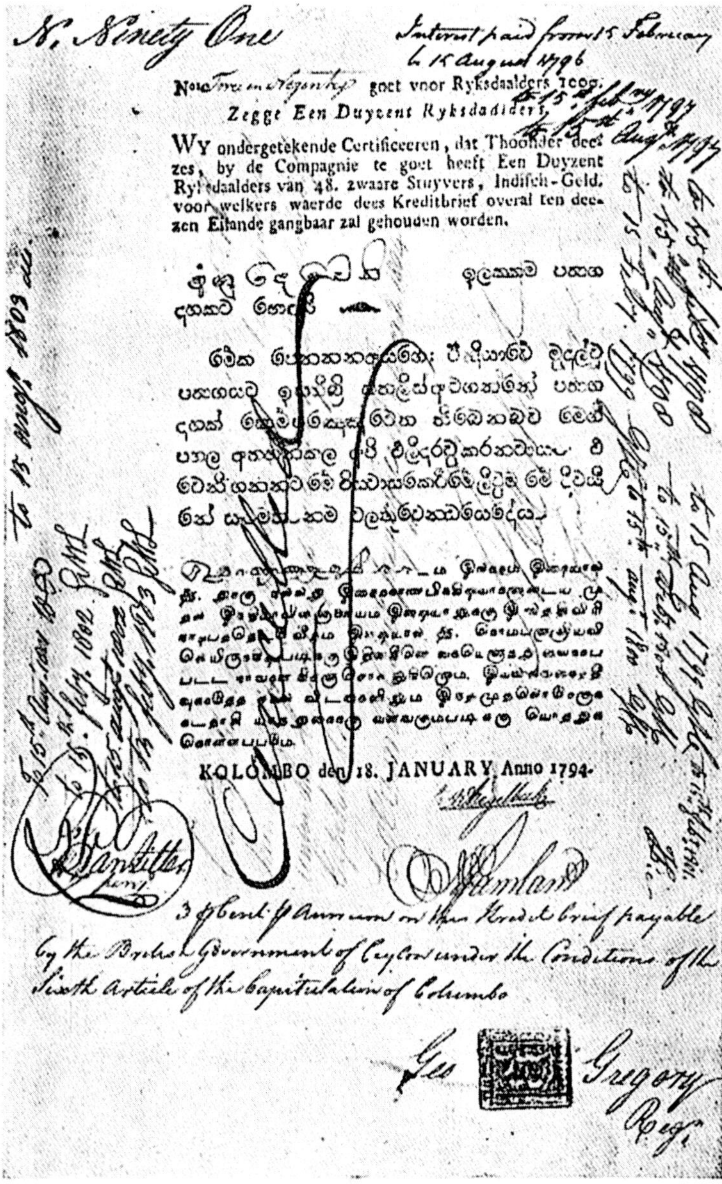

N. Ninety One

Interest paid from 15 February to 15 August 1796

No. .... goet voor Ryksdaalders 1000.

Zegge Een Duyzent Ryksdaalders.

WY ondergetekende Certificeeren, dat Thoonder dees zes, by de Compagnie te goet heeft Een Duyzent Ryksdaalders van 48. zwaare Stuyvers, Indisch-Geld, voor welkers waerde dees Kreditbrief overal ten deezen Eilande gangbaar zal gehouden worden.

KOLOMBO den 18. JANUARY Anno 1794.

3 p Cent p Annum on this Kredit brief payable by the British Government of Ceylon under the Conditions of the Sixth Article of the Capitulation of Columbo

Geo Gregory Regr.

SPECIMEN KREDIT BRIEF.

CEYLON CURRENCY—BRITISH PERIOD.

I.—1796-1824. FROM THE CAPITULATION OF COLOMBO TO THE ORDER IN COUNCIL INTRODUCING BRITISH CURRENCY.

Taking over of Dutch Currency—Introduction of English Copper.—The British occupied the maritime districts of Ceylon in 1795–6 and took possession of the Kandyan districts in 1815. In accordance with Article 6 of the Capitulation of Colombo they took over from the Dutch the promissory notes called Kredit Brieven (the first paper currency issued in Ceylon) which were then in circulation up to a limit of £50,000 and agreed to issue certificates for the amount bearing interest at the rate of 3 per cent. per annum payable half-yearly. The Dutch denominations were retained, the rixdollar being divided into 12 fanams=48 stuivers or pice=192 challies.

When the East India Company took over, the currency in Ceylon consisted of copper and paper. The rixdollar was an imaginary coin at the time merely used for keeping accounts, and the Arcot (or Madras) rupee, which was 12 fanams, was counted as the rixdollar. Before the British occupation the nominal value of this rupee was 30 stuivers though its real value was 48 or even higher.

The chief Indian standards at the time were the Star Pagoda and the Porto Novo Pagoda, both gold coins. The rate of exchange between these coins and the Ceylon currency, under the Dutch, was 1 Porto Novo Pagoda = 25½ fanams and 1 Star Pagoda = 30½ fanams. Under the British, the Indian currency increased in value relatively to the Ceylon stuiver. According to the Jaffna Diary the exchange on March 22, 1796, was 1 Porto Novo = 38½ fanams and 1 Star Pagoda = 45 fanams.

By Proclamation of June 8, 1796, currency was given to all Dutch copper coins, the stuiver to pass at 48 to the rixdollar or 180 to the Star Pagoda; the English copper also were to be current, the larger at one stuiver and the smaller at half stuiver.

2. **Coinage.**—The coins current during the early British period were :—

(i.) Copper: (*a*) Fanam or 1/12 rixdollar with its half and quarter minted locally, the quarter (otherwise known as the stuiver, pice or doodie), varying in weight from 205·2 grains to 140 grains; (*b*) double, single, half, and quarter stuiver pieces struck in England; (*c*) the Dutch coins, including the challies taken as prize money in Kandy and put into circulation in 1815 at 12 to the fanam; and (*d*) the English copper.

(ii.) Silver: (*a*) Rixdollar (double, single, and half)—each rixdollar weighing originally 152·5 grains, and later 140 grains minted locally, and the rixdollar of 1821 weighing 138⅔ grains struck in England; (*b*) Anchor Money—*i.e.*, silver fractions of the Spanish Dollar having on the reverse an anchor—(quarters, eighths, and sixteenths, weighing 104, 52, and 26 grains respectively), struck in England in 1820 and 1822; (*c*) Madras Rupees and Quarter Rupees—counter-marked in Ceylon with a Crown, declared current by Proclamation in 1823 at 1⅓ rixdollars and 4 fanams respectively; and (*d*) Fanam Tokens weighing 8·75 grains struck locally in 1814 and 1815.

Other coins in use were :—

	Value in 1803.		Value in 1822.						
	RD.	P.	*s.*	*d.*	or	RD.	F.	P.
Gold.								
Venetian ducat	6	24						
Bengal Muhr	22	0						
Surat Muhr	18	0						
Star Pagoda	5	0	8	0	=	4	6	3 3/7
Porto Novo Pagoda	4	0						
Tuticorin Pagoda	4	18						
Fanam (South India)								
Silver.								
Spanish Dollar (416 grs.)* ..	2	36	4	8	=	2	3	0
Surat (Bombay) Rupee (179 grs.)* ..	1	24						
†Sicca (Calcutta) Rupee (179 grs.)* ..	1	24	2	6	=	1	5	0 4/7
Arcot (Madras) Rupee (176 grs.)* ..	1	18	2	3½	=	1	3	2 5/7
Fanam (South India)								

The Government advertisement of July 4, 1817, rated copper as follows :—

	English.		Dutch.	
Challies ..	4	..	3	1 stuiver or pice
	16	..	12	1 fanam
	64	..	48	1 ridi
	192	..	144	1 rixdollar
Stuivers ..	4	..	—	1 fanam
	16	..	—	1 ridi
	48	..	—	1 rixdollar
Fanams ..	4	..	—	1 ridi
	12	..	—	1 rixdollar

3. **Minting of Coins.**—Coins (both silver and copper) were struck locally and also obtained from the Royal Mint in England.

(i.) **Copper: (*a*) Stuivers.**—The first coinage—pieces of 1, 2, and 4 stuivers—was struck locally in April 1801, by Adrian Peter Blume each stuiver weighing 205·2 grains. In 1802 the Royal Mint supplied whole, half, and quarter stuivers the average weight of a stuiver being 147 grains.

* Weights in 1800. † From the Arabic "Sicca" = coining die.

No. 2.

Obsolete Gold and Silver Coins.

SILVER FANAM.
(*South India*)

GOLD FANAM.
(*South India*)

STAR PAGODA.
(*South India*)

HALF RIXDOLLAR.

RIXDOLLAR.

TWO RIXDOLLAR PIECE.

* RIXDOLLAR STRUCK IN ENGLAND.

In 1805 a further quantity of stuivers (140 grains each) was struck in Colombo by Blume from a metal compound of 8 lb. of copper and 100 lb. of brass the latter obtained from old guns; and at Jaffna by one Chinnatamby from a mixture of 10 lb. of copper and 100 lb. of brass, each piece weighing 160·8 grains. The reason for the increased weight of the Jaffna stuiver is not known. In 1815 double, single, and half stuivers were struck at the Royal Mint on the basis of 50 stuivers to the pound.*

(*b*) **Pice.**—In March 1803 the Government provided 110,966 lb. of Japan copper to be coined into pice of the weight of 50 to the pound (*i.e.*, 140 grs. a piece), 44 to be delivered to Government and 6 to go to Blume to cover his expenses.

(ii.) **Silver : (*a*) Rixdollars.**—In 1803 Blume struck double, single, and half rixdollars, the rixdollar to be worth 20*d.* intrinsically but to be circulated at about 25½*d.*, each rixdollar of the first issue to weigh 152·5 grains and subsequent issues 140 grains, 10/12ths fine. In 1808–1809 double, single, and half rixdollars to the value of RD 692,000 approximately were coined by Blume of the same weight as the second issue of 1803 but with a reduced fineness. In 1822 owing to lack of metallic currency 400,000 rixdollars dated 1821 were obtained from the Royal Mint each weighing 138⅝ grains or one-third of a Spanish Dollar with a fineness of 891·6. This coin was intrinsically worth 1*s.* 6⅝*d.* at 4*s.* 8*d.* the Spanish Dollar but ordered to pass at 1*s.* 9*d.**

(*b*) **Anchor Money.**—In 1820 and 1822 silver fractions of the Spanish Dollar (quarters, eighths, and sixteenths) called "Anchor Money"—having on the reverse an anchor—were struck in England and sent to Ceylon.

(*c*) **Madras Rupees and Quarter Rupees.**—On March 22, and December 31, 1823, the Madras quarter and whole rupees, countermarked in Ceylon with a crown, were declared current by Proclamation at 4 fanams and 1⅓rd rixdollars respectively. 282,337 rupees and 260,000 quarter rupees were imported in 1823–24.

(*d*) **Fanams.**—2,095,467 fanams were minted in 1814–1815 locally at 12 to the rixdollar.

According to the Blue Book of 1824 the coins struck locally and in England were as follows :—

	RD
Silver struck locally, 1803–1809	981,030
Rixdollars of 1821	400,000
Copper struck locally	357,640
Copper struck in England	261,599

Until 1811 the local work was done on contract, the charges being 4 per cent. for silver and about 25 per cent. for copper. In 1811 contract work was stopped and a Mint established locally with A. Bertolacci in charge. The charges for copper were reduced to about 11 per cent. Copper coins were minted in Ceylon till 1816.

* For details of coins struck between 1801 and 1817 see pp. 154–157 "Ceylon Coins and Currency" by H. W. Codrington.

4. **Exchange.**—The East India Company had fixed the value of the Star Pagoda at 45 fanams or 180 stuivers. The value of coins, however, varied from time to time, and at different places. In 1802 the Star Pagoda was reckoned as RD 4 or 48 fanams. It was actually RD 5 or 60 fanams in 1807; 70 fanams in 1809, and 80 fanams in 1813. The rixdollar was equal to 12 Ceylon fanams. The actual worth of the rixdollar (silver at 62*d*. per oz.) was just over 1*s*. 6*d*., yet in 1804–05 it was officially rated at 2*s*. 1 3/5*d* Proclamation of March 13, 1812, rated the rixdollar at 1*s*. 9*d*., the reason assigned being that the rixdollar was originally valued with reference to the Star Pagoda and at a rate higher than its intrinsic value.

The Colonial Treasury issued bills on London for rixdollars at their nominal and not real value; and bills on Madras at 48 fanams or RD 4 for a Star Pagoda. The loss was only about 6 per cent. on the exchange into sterling. So long as bills were granted at the fixed rates no Ceylon coin was exported, but in 1805 on instructions from the Secretary of State the Government refused to accept from public servants rixdollars in silver, copper, or paper at the official value, declined to issue bills as before, but disposed of them to the highest bidder. The result was that the whole currency fell to the intrinsic value of its coins, and by 1809 practically all the silver, and by 1811 a good part of the copper, the oldest and heaviest, had left the Island. The depreciation of the coinage, and its scarcity, the rise in exchange and an unfavourable balance of trade brought about general distress and ruined commerce during the period 1811 to 1813.

Between 1815 and 1819 the exchange was RD 5 and RD 4 for a Star Pagoda and a Porto Novo respectively. In 1819, fanams 54 6/7 went to the Star Pagoda, 17 1/7 to the Sicca Rupee, and 15 33/49 to the Arcot Rupee. From this time the Ceylon fanam practically and, in 1823 actually, equalled the Indian anna. Towards the end of 1824 the exchange was about RD 15 to the £1.

5. **Paper Currency.**—The first issue of paper currency by the British was made in March, 1800, the notes being generally of the denominations of RD 100, 50, and 25 and redeemable in current coin. The history of paper currency is described in detail in Part II.

6. **Counterfeiting, Commission, and Discount.**—Regulation 12 of 1814 imposed penalties for counterfeiting coins which were current. In spite of this the coinage was still being counterfeited and Regulation 11 of 1824 was issued imposing further penalties. By Regulation 18 of 1822 it was made illegal to receive or pay for any silver or copper coin or Government notes any more in value, benefit or advantage, than the true lawful value, except lawful discount on such notes as were not expressed to be payable on demand.

7. **Public Accounts.**—The accounts were kept until 1302 in Star Pagodas, divided into Madras fanams and cash*, or into Ceylon fanams

* According to the monetary scheme in Madras at the time 80 copper cash = 1 silver fanam; 12 fanams = 1 rupee; 3½ rupees = 1 star pagoda.

and challies, as well as in rixdollars, fanams, and challies. In 1802 Ceylon came under the direct control of the Secretary of State for the Colonies and thereafter the accounts were kept in rixdollars, fanams, and pice instead of Star Pagodas, the rixdollar being rated at quarter of a Pagoda or 2 shillings.

II.—1825-1868. FROM THE ORDER IN COUNCIL INTRODUCING BRITISH CURRENCY TO THE ORDER IN COUNCIL CONSTITUTING THE "COMPANY'S" RUPEE AND ITS SILVER SUBDIVISIONS THE ONLY LEGAL TENDER IN CEYLON.

8. **1825—Introduction of British Silver. Public Accounts in £. s. d.**—In 1825 the Home Government decided to introduce British silver coins into all the Colonial possessions with the object of providing "an unobjectionable and unvarying medium for the payment of troops and of establishing a uniform currency in the whole of His Majesty's Foreign possessions founded upon and having reference to the currency of the United Kingdom". By Order in Council of March 23, 1825 (Appendix A), and Regulation 8 of July 4, 1825*, British silver was declared legal tender for the payment of any amount, as also were the silver rixdollars of 1821 and the paper rixdollars at the rate of 1*s.* 6*d.* each. British copper viz., pence, half-pence, and farthings, and the copper coins of the Island viz., fanam at 1½*d.*, half-fanam at ¾*d.*, pice at ⅜*d.*, half-pice at 3/16*d.*, and the Dutch challie at ⅛*d.*, were made legal tender to the extent of 1 shilling. Regulation 8 further ordained that thenceforth all Government Accounts in Ceylon should be kept in pounds, shillings and pence.

It was also notified that bills on London at 3 days' sight would be exchanged by the Government for sums of not less than £100, at the fixed rate of £100 sterling = £103 of either British silver money, paper or silver rixdollars paid into the Colonial Treasury.

9. **Spanish Dollars and Indian Rupees.**—If the Governor required any sum beyond the amount so paid into the Treasury at the prescribed rates he was further authorized to negotiate his bills for Spanish dollars, Indian rupees, or other coin at the best terms he could obtain and issue them at their intrinsic value as compared to British standard silver at 5*s.* 2*d.* an oz. At this rate Spanish and American dollars were valued at 4*s.* 4*d.*, the Sicca rupee at 2*s.* 1*d.*, and Bombay and Surat rupees at 1*s.* 11*d.* These coins had been overvalued, compared with the then market price of silver and the British silver in its representative capacity, to the extent of nearly 4 per cent.; and the error was later rectified by Minute of December 14, 1833, which fixed the value of a Spanish dollar at 4*s.* 2*d.*, Sicca rupee at 2*s.*, and Madras and Bombay rupee at 1*s.* 10*d.*

10. **1825–1833. Cancellation of Paper Rixdollars and Issue of Sterling Notes.**—In the years 1825 to 1833 the Government imported British silver to the value of £111,895 while during the same period Government bills on London were disposed of to the extent of £1,521,784. The

* *Supplement to the Ceylon Gazette,* dated Saturday, 2nd July, 1825.

paper rixdollars paid in were all cancelled and a new paper currency to the extent of about £90,000 expressed in terms of sterling was issued under Regulation 8 of 1827. This enacted that Government notes expressed in pounds payable in the currency of the Island shall pass current at 20 shillings sterling. The notes were payable at the Treasury in specie on demand but the holders were not allowed the right given to the holders of the old inconvertible rixdollar paper of exchanging them for bills on London at the fixed rate of premium.

Regulation 6 of 1830 demonetized as from January 1, 1831, all copper coins struck in Ceylon and then current.

11. **1833–1836. Failure of attempt to introduce and circulate British Coins in Ceylon.**—After 1833 no importation of British silver appears to have taken place. Although British silver coins and rixdollars continued to be the only legal tender and the accounts were kept in terms of British money, the object of "establishing a currency for the Colony founded upon and having reference to the currency of the United Kingdom" and the scheme for retaining it in the Island by means of a fixed rate of exchange were both defeated by the fluctuations of Indian exchange for which no allowance had been made. Government was obliged to sell its bills on India, frequently at very unfavourable rates, and to import and put into circulation the proceeds which consisted of Indian rupees which were not legal tender. In the period 1834 to 1836 rupees to the value of £141,136 were imported by Government from India and issued at the rates fixed in 1833. The rupees so imported did not remain long in circulation but were re-exported to India owing to fluctuations in exchange and in consequence of the Island's unfavourable balance of trade. It was considered at the time that the difficulty of retaining the coin in the Island arose from the undervaluation of the rupee as compared with its exchange value, the rupee being then worth for exchange on London from 2*d*., to 2½*d*., above its intrinsic value.

12. **1836–1850. Disappearance of British Silver and Rixdollars. Introduction of "Company's" Rupee.**—The Madras and Bombay rupee of 180 grains, 11/12ths fine, was by the Indian Act of August, 1835, No. XVII, adopted as the standard rupee for the whole of India and was styled the "Company's" rupee*. The intrinsic value of this coin was 1*s*. 10⅝*d*., silver at 5*s*. per oz., but it cost the Government from 2*s*. to 2*s*. 0½*d*. in India in exchange for its bills on London plus a further charge for freight and insurance; and although not legal tender, it was issued to the Civil and Military Establishments at 1*s*. 10*d*. under the terms of the Minute of December 14, 1833. In order to counteract the flow of coin from the Island the Governor issued a Minute dated September 26, 1836, giving notice that the Company's rupee will be put in circulation in

* The weight and fineness of this coin have remained unaltered but in 1862 (by Act No. XIII.) the crowned effigy of the Queen was introduced and the name of the coin was declared to be the "Government" rupee. The coins which do not bear as device the head of the reigning sovereign are not legal tender.

No. 3.

A RIXDOLLAR NOTE.

future at 2*s.*, ½ rupee at 1*s.*, and ¼ rupee at 6*d.* This effected a complete revolution in the currency system of the Island although it entirely failed in accomplishing the object for which it was designed.

By the Minute of September 26, 1836, the Company's rupee was over-rated relatively to British sterling to the extent of over 7½ per cent. It became practically the standard of value, and British silver and rix-dollars which were undervalued relatively to the rupee naturally disappeared after a time from circulation, their place being taken by the over-valued rupee. The effect of the Minute was merely to depreciate the value of the metallic currency of the Island while it proved entirely powerless to arrest the exportation of the coin.

Thus after an ineffectual attempt to establish in the Colony the currency of the United Kingdom, and after a series of mistakes, the result produced was the assimilation of the currency of Ceylon with that of India. This was the natural order of things, considering the intimate economic and social relations existing between the two countries which may be considered geographically as one.

13. **1851–1868. English and Australian Gold coins introduced. Rupee and its subdivisions in actual use.**—In 1851 the local Government requested the sanction of the Home authorities to a suggestion by the Chamber of Commerce, Colombo, to increase the currency of the Colony by the addition of British gold coins. The Lords Commissioners of the Treasury ruled that a local ordinance was not necessary to give currency within the Island to the gold coins of the Realm which, as being issued from Her Majesty's Mint under Her Royal authority, were a legal discharge for the sums they represented throughout Her Majesty's dominions. This ruling was, however, subsequently considered incorrect, and an Order in Council and a Proclamation, both dated October 16, 1852, were issued declaring that the coins of the United Kingdom (viz., sovereigns, half-sovereigns, &c.) shall pass current in Ceylon, but reducing the legal tender limit of British silver to 40 shillings (Appendix B). In 1856 by Order in Council and Proclamation dated October 22 Australian gold coins too were made legal tender in Ceylon (Appendix B).

The rupee and its subdivisions, however, continued to be the coins in actual use throughout the Island, though not legal tender. The Minute of September 26, 1836, was considered *ultra vires* as it was not within the power of the Governor to declare a coin legal tender by a mere Government notification, such a step to be valid requiring an Order in Council and a Royal Proclamation or a Legislative enactment confirmed by the Crown. Clause 5 of "The Coining Prevention Ordinance" (No. 5 of 1857) enacted, "that for the purpose of the Ordinance the Company's rupee, half-rupee, and quarter-rupee shall be deemed to be silver coins lawfully current in this Colony"; but in as much as this Ordinance did not declare the rupee a silver coin lawfully current in the Colony "for all purposes", but only provided that "it shall be deemed to be such for the purposes of the said Ordinance ", it was considered that the legal effect of it was simply to constitute the counterfeiting of the rupee an offence, but that it did not make it a legal tender. It was for this reason that the principal bank in the Island viz : the Oriental Bank Corporation endeavoured to guard itself against any inconvenience or loss by issuing its notes expressed in rupees. The notes of the Chartered Mercantile Bank and those of the Asiatic Banking Corporation were expressed in " Pounds " of " the currency of the Island ".

III.—1869-1892. FROM THE ORDER IN COUNCIL OF 1869 TO THE ORDER IN COUNCIL OF 1892. THE RUPEE OF BRITISH INDIA CONSTITUTED AS THE STANDARD COIN OF CEYLON WITH A SUBSIDIARY DECIMAL COINAGE.

14. **Disappearance of Paper currency, Rixdollars, English and Australian coins except British Copper. Legalization of the " Company's " Rupee.**—The sterling notes issued under the authority of Regulation 8 of 1827 had been cancelled periodically as they were received at the local Treasuries and only about £1,000 worth of them were outstanding in 1865. These were treated as " not in existence ". British silver coins and rixdollars had long since disappeared and sovereigns, both English and Australian, were not in circulation. Although the rupee had for many years been the universally recognized measure of value the fact that it was not current under " legal " authority, though not generally known, was a disturbing factor. In order to remove permanently this legal uncertainty, Order in Council and Proclamation dated June 18, 1869 (brought into operation on January 1, 1872, by Proclamation of August 23, 1871), were issued (Appendices C and D).

Order in Council of June 18, 1869, revoked Order in Council dated March 23, 1825, and so much of the Orders in Council of October 16, 1852, and October 22, 1856, as had effect in the Island, and repealed Regulations 8 of 1825 and 8 of 1827.

It was declared that the British and local copper or bronze coins then in circulation and such other copper or bronze tokens as may from time to time be specified by the Governor by Proclamation shall be legal tender for any sum not exceeding half a rupee—a penny to be current at $\frac{2}{3}$ anna, $\frac{1}{2}$ penny at $\frac{1}{3}$ anna, farthing at $\frac{1}{6}$ anna, Ceylon fanam at 1 anna, stuiver or pice at $\frac{1}{4}$ anna, and challie at 1/12 anna.

It was further ordained and declared that the Company's silver rupee of 180 grains, 11/12 fine, and its silver subdivisions ($\frac{1}{2}$, $\frac{1}{4}$, and $\frac{1}{8}$ rupee) shall be the only legal tender in Ceylon and its Dependencies.*

* Silver rupees issued from the Indian Mints from 1835 to 1869 consisted of 4 issues, viz., one in 1835, two in 1840, and one in 1862 ; and were coined at Calcutta, Madras, and Bombay. The 1835 issue has the uncrowned effigy of William IV., and the two issues in 1840 the uncrowned effigy of Queen Victoria. These 3 issues have the words " East India Company " on the reverse. The coins of 1862 bear the crowned effigy of the Queen but not the name of the Company. Although these issues are still legal tender they are withdrawn from circulation whenever they are received at a Government Treasury in India.

It was also declared that whenever the denomination of British Currency shall have been specified in any Regulation, Ordinance, Minute, &c., or Contract in force at the date of the Proclamation of the Order in Council in Ceylon, such sums, whether as payments to be made to or by the local Government, shall continue to be received at and paid from the local Treasuries in rupees and the legal subordinate currency of the Island at 2 shillings to the rupee.

15. **A decimal coinage proposed.**—In September, 1869 after the publication of the Order in Council making the "Company's" rupee and its silver subdivisions the only legal tender in the Island, the then Director of Public Works (Mr. Guilford L. Molesworth) submitted a report advocating the introduction of a subsidiary decimal coinage of the rupee. He proposed that the rupee, half-rupee, and quarter rupee should remain in circulation, that the rupee should be subdivided into 100 units, termed cents, and that the following subsidiary coins be introduced, viz., silver ten cents, and copper five, two, one, and half cents. There was also a proposal that Government Accounts should be kept on a rupee instead of a sterling basis.

16. **A triangular contest: Chamber of Commerce supports £. s. d. Commission recommend Rupees, Annas, Pies. The Public favour Rupees and Cents.**—The proposed changes in the currency system, especially the proposal to keep public accounts in rupees, were vehemently opposed by the Chamber of Commerce, Colombo, who contended that the contemplated change was inexpedient, and if carried into effect would cause serious inconvenience to the mercantile, agricultural, and trading communities and great dissatisfaction to the public. A Commission was immediately appointed by the Governor with Hon. Mr. George Lawson, Puisne Judge, as Chairman, to consider and report whether any change would become either necessary or desirable in the denomination of the Public Accounts in view of the Order in Council declaring the rupee the legal tender of payment. The Commission recommended, by a majority, the adoption of the Indian System of rupees, annas, and pies.

17. **Rupees and Cents adopted.**—A minority of the Commission, however, led by Sir Richard Morgan, Queen's Advocate, Mr. Molesworth, Director of Public Works, and Mr. T. Berwick, District Judge, strongly urged the adoption of a decimal coinage. This was followed by the formation of "A Decimal Association" and by further representations in support of the decimal system, one hundred and eleven petitions being presented to the Governor. A cogent reason urged in its favour was that the decimal coinage was not new to the Sinhalese. After a protracted correspondence for over 18 months between the Colonial Office and the Lords Commissioners of the Treasury, Sir Hercules Robinson received the assent of the Secretary of State in June, 1871, to the adoption of a decimal subdivision of the rupee and the introduction of the copper five, one, and half cent pieces according to the design submitted by the Governor in January, 1870

the arrangement to take effect from January 1, 1872. From this date the Accounts of the Colony have been kept in rupees and cents.

18. **Rating of Copper. Introduction of quarter cent piece. Demonetization of the Fanam, Stuiver, and Challie.**—Pending the introduction of the decimal tokens the following coins were rated as below by Proclamation dated August 23, 1871 (Appendix D) :—

Penny = 1/24 rupee or ⅔ anna
Half penny = 1/48 ,, ⅓ ,,
Farthing = 1/96 ,, ⅙ ,,
Ceylon fanam = 1/16 rupee or 1 anna.
Stuiver or pice = 1/64 rupee or ¼ anna.
Challie = 1/192 rupee or 1/12 anna or 1 pie.

Quarter cent pieces were introduced on September 14, 1872*. Proclamation of March 17, 1874, demonetized the fanam, stuiver, and challie.

19. **Re-establishment of State Note Issue.**—The Sterling Notes issued by Government in 1827 were withdrawn as from 1856, the Kachcheries being permitted to accept notes issued by the Oriental Bank Corporation in payment of Government dues. This bank failed on May 3, 1884, due mostly to speculation, and the Secretary of State rather reluctantly gave his approval to the re-establishment of a Government Note Issue expressed in rupees. The present issue is regulated by Ordinance No. 32 of 1884 (Appendix L.)

20. **Introduction of a local subsidiary silver coinage. Proposal to demonetize Indian Small Silver.**—On December 19, 1889, the Legislative Council adopted a resolution as follows :—" That the Government do take steps to remedy the inconvenience and loss sustained by the public, especially the poorer classes, by the anomalous position in the currency of the Indian 2 anna piece ".

In view of the fact that the Government of India would not mint its own small coins for export without limit, and the anomaly of having for a decimal coinage coins of 25 and 12½ cents, and the condemnation by the Legislative Council unanimously of the silver 2 anna piece the Executive Council recommended the demonetization of the Indian silver pieces of 2, 4, and 8 annas and the introduction of a complete subsidiary silver coinage.

21. **Legal tender limit and fineness of the proposed coinage.**—As regards the limit of tender and the fineness, the Auditor-General and the Treasurer observed that the reason for preferring a low touch to a high one was that coins of a low touch stood the ordinary wear and tear better ; and further, the lower the touch the larger would be the profit to Government ; but on the other hand the lower the intrinsic value of a coinage the greater would be the temptation for fraud by counterfeiting. In view of the fact that the limit of legal tender would depend on the fineness of the coins they did

* The quarter cent piece was called in by Proclamation dated December 13, 1909 (Appendix H).

No. 4.

Obsolete Copper Coins.

FANAM = 1/12 RIXDOLLAR.

HALF FANAM = 1/24 RD.

STUIVER OR QUARTER FANAM = 1/48 RD.

ENGLISH CHALLIE OR QUARTER STUIVER = 1/192 RD
STRUCK AT THE ROYAL MINT.

DUTCH CHALLIE = 1/144 RD.

not consider any limit necessary if the fineness was, like the Indian small silver, the same as in the rupee (*i.e.*, 916·6̇). But if the lower fineness of four-fifths was to be adopted as in the case of the Straits Settlements and Mauritius, they suggested a five rupee limit. In these circumstances, it was decided to propose a 4/5th fineness and a legal tender limit of five rupees for the Ceylon subsidiary silver coinage.

The Financial Advisers to the Government were of opinion that these changes could be effected by a local enactment, and they further proposed that the rupee of Portuguese India should also be legalized as it was legal tender at Tuticorin. The Secretary of State, however, pointed out that as these proposals would affect the Order in Council of June 18, 1869, an instrument assented to by the Queen was necessary, and he agreed to take the necessary steps to give effect to the proposals. The Government of India whilst having no objection to the changes proposed stated that the Indian half-rupee was not a subsidiary coin but full legal tender for any amount, and that it was willing to mint the required silver coins at Calcutta provided they were of the rupee standard of 11/12th fineness and not of a lower touch. The proposal to demonetize all the Indian small silver coins was therefore modified, as it was felt to be inadvisable to dispense with the Indian half rupee, a coin which was full legal tender. It was also urged that the demonetization of the silver 4 and 8 anna pieces would seriously inconvenience the holders of these coins in Ceylon, especially the poor and illiterate villagers, and cause hardship to the Indian immigrants proceeding to Ceylon. As regards the silver 2 anna piece, however, in view of the unanimous vote in the Legislative Council condemning it, it was decided to withdraw it, and issue in its place a silver coin of the value of 10 cents ; also to retain the Indian ¼ and ½ rupees concurrently with the proposed new 25 and 50 cent pieces, leaving the local coins of lower touch to oust the Indian coinage of higher fineness. The silver 2 anna piece was accordingly abandoned in 1891.

22. **Order in Council issued.**—The Lords Commissioners of the Treasury approved these proposals and an Order in Council dated February 6, 1892 (Appendix E), was issued rescinding the Order in Council and Proclamation dated June 18, 1869, and repealing "all such Colonial laws and all such proclamations whether issued by Her Majesty or by the Governor, as regulate legal tender in the Colony other than the Paper Currency Ordinance, 1884", and declaring *inter alia* that—

(i.) The silver rupee of British India of the standard weight of 180 grains (11·664 grammes) and millesimal fineness of 916·6̇, the least current weight being 176·4 grains (11·431 grammes), shall be the standard coin of Ceylon and its dependencies ; and that the silver rupee of Portuguese India having the same weight and fineness shall be treated as equal to the standard coin*.

* The Indo-Portuguese rupee was demonetized as from July 19, 1893, by Order in Council of July 17, published in Ceylon on August 17, 1893 (Appendix F).

(ii.) (*a*) Subsidiary coins may be from time to time coined for the Colony under the direction of the Master of the Royal Mint or at one of Her Majesty's Mints in British India of the denominations, weights, and fineness specified below, each coin to be a legal tender for the amount of its denomination :—

Coin.	Metal.	Millesimal fineness.	Standard wt. in grs.	Remedy wt. grains.	allowances fineness.
Cents 50	Silver	800	90	·630	3
25	"	800	45	·315	3
10	"	800	18	·18	3
05*	Copper or Mixed Metal	—	291·6̇	7·29	None
01	Copper or Mixed Metal	—	72·916	1·82	"
0½	Copper or Mixed Metal	—	36·458	0·91	"
0¼	Copper or Mixed Metal	—	18·229	0·46	"

(*b*) Each of the following Indian silver coins to be legal tender as shown below :—

	Fineness.	Std. wt.	Least current wt.
½ rupee or 8 anna	916·6̇	90 grs.	88·2 grs.
¼ rupee or 4 anna	916·6̇	45 "	44·1 "

½ rupee and ¼ rupee to be legal tender for cents 50 and 25 respectively.

(iii.) Provided that the coins have not been illegally dealt with, and provided that, in the case of silver coins, such coins have not become diminished in weight by wear or otherwise so as to be of less weight than the weight (if any) specified as the least current weight, they shall be a legal tender :—

(*a*) in the case of rupees, for the payment of any amount ;

(*b*) in the case of other silver coins, for the payment of an amount not exceeding five rupees ;

(*c*) in the case of coins of copper or mixed metal for the payment of an amount not exceeding half a rupee.

(iv.) If the Governor from time to time requests any new coins of less value than the rupee, whether of silver, copper, or mixed metal to be coined and the Commissioners of the Treasury approve, these new coins may be coined at one of the Mints mentioned above, and such new coin may be of the same denomination as any existing coin, or of a different denomination ; and, if of silver shall be of the same fineness as the existing silver coins, and of a weight bearing the same proportion to the weights of the existing silver coins as the denomination of the new coin bears to the denominations of the existing coins.

(v.) A coin shall be deemed to have been illegally dealt with where the coin has been impaired, diminished, or lightened otherwise than by fair wear and tear, or has been defaced by having any name, word, or

* Nickel-bronze with 60 grains as standard weight substituted by Proclamation of December 13, 1909 (Appendix I).

device, or number stamped thereon, whether the coin has or has not been thereby diminished or lightened.*

(vi.) This Order shall come into operation on the 1st day of July, 1892, and may be cited as " The Coinage (Ceylon) Order, 1892 ".

The Order in Council was proclaimed on June 23, 1892, to take effect from and after July 1, 1892, but the delay in the arrival of the new coins, viz., silver 10, 25, and 50 cents, necessitated the date for its operation to be altered to October 1, 1892, by an Amending Order in Council dated June 28, 1892, published in Ceylon on July 21, 1892.

23. **English Copper too disappear.**—With the proclamation of " The Coinage (Ceylon) Order, 1892 ", the English copper which had been current in the Island since the beginning of British rule also ceased to be legal tender.

24. **Coins minted.**—During the period 1870–1892, 41,014,143 one cent pieces and 32,328,000 half cent pieces were obtained from the Royal Mint. All the coins supplied on indents from 1870 to 1889 appear to have been dated 1870.

IV.—1893–1903. THE SILVER CRISIS. APPOINTMENT OF TWO CURRENCY COMMISSIONS.

(i.) *The First Commission, when India put an artificial value on the silver rupee.*

25. **Silver rupee and its gold value.**—Silver rupees which were current in India had been in use in Ceylon from about the year 1676 although the " Company's " rupee was made legal tender only with effect from January 1, 1872†. The Order in Council of June 18, 1869, rated the rupee at 2 shillings. Until 1893 the currency of India was on the basis of silver freely minted, the gold value of the rupee fluctuating with the gold value of silver bullion. The Government of India were bound by the Coinage Act of 1870 to issue rupees, weight for weight, in exchange for silver bullion. From about 1873 the price of silver stated in terms of gold fell steadily, and early in June 1893 the rupee was only worth 1*s*. 2⅝*d*. On June 26, 1893, the Indian Government fixed the value of the rupee at 1*s*. 4*d*. and, in order to make the value of the rupee approximate to that rate by rendering the coin more scarce, it closed the mints to the free coinage of rupees and withheld the sale of Council Bills.

Commission appointed.

This action of the Indian Government led to the appointment of the Ceylon Silver Currency Commission, consisting of the Auditor-General

---

* Defaced coins are not legal tender. Defacement includes clipping, filing, stamping or such other alteration on the surface or in the shape of a coin as is readily distinguishable from the effects of reasonable wear. " Government of India Resource Manual, 1938."

† Bengal Regulation XXXV. of 1793 specifies no less than 27 varieties of rupees.

(Hon. Mr. James A. Swettenham), as Chairman, the Treasurer, the Principal Collector of Customs, the Chairman of the Chamber of Commerce, the Chairman of the Planters' Association, and four others. The Commission was asked to consider and report as to—

(1) the probable effect in Ceylon of the action of the Indian Government in putting an artificial value on the rupee ; and

(2) the measures which it may be expedient to take to protect the interests of the Colony under the altered nature of the currency.

Commission's findings.

26. (*a*) **Effect of falling rate of exchange.**—After a careful examination of the evidence and the statistics collected, the Commission found that during the preceding 20 years (1873 to 1893) while the gold price of silver had been falling, the effect of the fall had been as follows :—

Mercantile interests.—As far as the merchants' interests were concerned the local merchant had had a greater volume of business owing to the progressive increase of exports and to the increase of shipping calling at Colombo ; on the other hand, he had suffered from the harassing influence of a constantly fluctuating exchange and the drawback of the shrinkage of capital engaged in business, when measured in terms of gold.

Producers' interests.—The European and native owners of estates whose expenditure was largely on unskilled labour had benefited by the low exchange. The circumstances of the ordinary labourer who had little or no property had varied very much in different parts of the Island. The standard of living of labourers had increased generally and wages had risen in many districts.

Immigrants' interests.—As regards immigrant labourers they did not appear to have received any direct benefit from falling exchange, and could only have benefited through the prosperity of the employer enabling him to offer employment to a larger number of immigrants.

English Civilians' interests.—The fall in exchange had brought on the English Civil Servants two distinct sources of hardship : (i.) the process of falling and (ii.) the permanently low value of the rupee. The losses under the first source had been considerable amongst the senior Civil Servants who paid insurance premia and contributions to funds in rupees which were on the average of a very much higher sterling value than would be obtained when the object of the payments came to be realized ; and any sums of money saved and retained in the Colony with the ultimate intention of being transferred to Europe on retirement were now of much less value in sterling than they originally were.

Government interests.—As far as the Government was concerned, the increase of revenue had been accompanied by an increase in the gold debt and gold payments. The prosperity of the producing interests was the main cause of the satisfactory condition of Colonial Revenue, and if that prosperity were materially checked by a change in currency which also effected a saving to the Government on its gold obligations, the direct saving so effected might not be a sufficient compensation for the probable shrinkage of revenue.

General position.—As regards the general position of Ceylon and its trade, the statistics pointed to a general increase of prosperity during the period when the fall of the rupee was most marked. The evidence was conclusive that that fall had not prevented the introduction of all necessary English capital: in fact, there was more capital offering for investment on reasonable terms than had ever been the case before.

(*b*) **Effect of raising gold value.**—The Commission was of opinion that up to the present time a bullion silver currency, coupled with a falling rate of exchange, had been for the benefit of the greatest number, and that the sum of the advantages had preponderated over the sum of the disadvantages; but that, as far as they could see, the action of the Government of India in putting an artificial value on the rupee was not advantageous to the general interests of Ceylon.

The Commissioners did not think that a gradual and moderate rise in the sterling value of the rupee would, if equally felt by the currencies of other silver using countries, seriously affect the prosperity of the Colony; but the effect of the action of the Indian Government in fixing the rate of exchange at 1*s*. 4*d*. had so far not been to raise the value of the rupee (except for a short period of speculation) above its pre-existing value, but to create a great divergence between the token currency value and the bullion value of the coin (on June 1, 1893, the divergence was 1/32*d*. but on February 8, 1894, it had risen to 2¾*d*.), and it was this divergence in values which they feared would menace the prosperity of some of the Island's staple products. There was no doubt that, if this divergence were large, Ceylon products would only retain their markets by accepting prices so low as to seriously imperil the prosperity of the largest producing classes in the Island. The growing divergence between bullion value and the scarcity value of the rupee would also offer an ever-increasing temptation to illicit coinage.

27. **Future effects.**—As regards the future, the Commission was of opinion that 3 things might happen to the value of silver measured in terms of gold: (1) it might remain stationary; (2) it might diminish; or (3) it might increase. The effect upon Ceylon, if she were to take no independent action in each of these 3 cases, the Commission considered would be as follows:—

In the first case, producers of tea and coconuts would be handicapped as regards rivals in silver standard countries. In the second case, Ceylon producers would be still handicapped to the extent to which the action of the Indian Government was successful in raising the value of the rupee above the value of the pure silver contained in it. In the third case, the disadvantage to Ceylon would tend constantly to diminish until it disappeared entirely.

28. **What measures it may be expedient to take to protect the interests of the Colony under the altered nature of the currency.**—After discussing the remedies proposed, viz.: (*a*) International bimetallism, (*b*) a coin of commerce, and (*c*) a Ceylon rupee, the Commission reported that (*a*) seemed impossible at the time as all nations would not agree; as regards (*b*), the subject had already been decided upon by a Royal Commission in 1868 in favour of the British sovereign or the pound sterling; and as regards (*c*), the Government of India had telegraphed to the Secretary of State on March 16, 1893, that Ceylon must not be allowed to coin in her own mints new rupees resembling the Indian rupee; and Lord Herchell's Committee (1893–1894) had decided that Colonial Governments should not allow any coin which they issue to be so similar to the Indian rupee as to be mistaken for it.

29. **Conclusion.**—In these circumstances, the Commission was of opinion that a change of currency would be profitable only if silver fell still lower, but disadvantageous in every other case; and in regard to the possibility of Ceylon obtaining rice and other supplies from silver standard countries instead of India, they came to the conclusion that while the course of trade might turn against India, Ceylon must still remain largely indebted to India in that respect. The Commission was therefore unable to advise the Government of Ceylon to sever its connection with the currency of India, as the risks inseparable from such a change were as great as, if not greater than, those which might be expected from inaction at the present time.

(ii.) *The Second Commission, when the reintroduction of gold caused a scarcity of silver.*

30. **Sovereign again made legal tender.**—English and Australian gold coins were first declared legal tender in Ceylon by Orders in Council dated October 16, 1852, and October 22, 1856, respectively. These Orders were revoked by the Order in Council of June 18, 1869, which ordained that the "Company's" rupee and its silver subdivisions "shall be the sole legal tender" The Indian Coinage and Paper Currency Act of 1899 had made gold legal tender in India and, as there was an obvious advantage in being able to retain a portion of the Currency Note Reserve in coin with an intrinsic value and small bulk such as the sovereign rather than in coin of artificial value and large bulk like the rupee, an Order in Council dated September 26, 1901, was issued constituting the sovereign a legal tender again in the Island at the rate of Rs. 15 a sovereign, and was brought into force with effect from October 25, 1901, by Proclamation of the same date (Appendix G).

31. **Importation of silver rupees discontinued by banks, causing scarcity of silver. A Commission appointed.**—When Ordinance No. 13 of 1901 was passed permitting the Commissioners of Currency to receive gold as well as silver in exchange for currency notes, the banks found that they could import gold coins at about 1/16 per cent. cheaper (the rate for gold being about 3/16 per cent. and the rate for silver ¼ per cent.), and they practically discontinued the importation of silver. Their action caused heavy demands on the stock of silver in the hands of the Commissioners. The silver reserve fell during 1902 from over 5 million rupees to less than 2 millions while the gold in the reserve rose to over 6 million rupees. The scarcity of silver was injuriously affecting trade and causing alarm, and it became a matter of considerable anxiety. On 5th November, 1902, the Government appointed a Commission with the Attorney-General (Hon. Mr. A. G. Lascelles) as Chairman to inquire into and report on the existing scarcity of silver in the Colony and to suggest some way of meeting the present difficulty and of preventing its recurrence.

Commission's recommendations.

32. (i.) **To meet the existing difficulty.**—The Commission recommended the immediate importation of 20 lacs of rupees by Government from India in exchange for gold in the reserve, and suggested that it would be advisable to amend local ordinances by providing explicitly that gold in transit from Ceylon for the purpose of exchanging for rupees, and rupees in transit for Ceylon, may be regarded for the purpose of the Currency Ordinance as a part of the Commissioners' reserve.

(ii.) **To meet future scarcity.**—The proposals put forward with a view to prevent a future scarcity of silver were—

(1) Repeal of Ordinance No. 13 of 1901; or its modification by either (*a*) limitation of the gold reserve, or (*b*) giving the Commissioners the option of issuing or refusing to issue currency notes in exchange for gold.

(2) Imposition of an import duty on sovereigns.

(3) Prohibition of importation of sovereigns from India.

(4) Increase of subsidiary coinage and raising the limit of its legal tender.

(5) Issue of notes of smaller value than Rs. 5.

(6) Importation of rupees by Government.

(7) Allowing the present situation to continue.

(8) Minting of a Ceylon rupee, its advantages being that—

(*a*) it would make Ceylon independent of India for her currency;

(*b*) it would render unnecessary the bringing down from India of Indian rupees;

(c) it would bring a handsome profit to Government; and

(d) it would be on a stronger basis than the Indian rupee, if absolutely convertible with gold.

The Commission considered (2) and (3) unworkable; (4) and (5) inadequate; and (6) and (7) impolitic. As regards (1) and (8), while admitting the advantages which would ensue if the Colony had a separate rupee coin which would remain in the Island, the Commission was not prepared to recommend its adoption until the question was thoroughly investigated by competent authorities outside the Island, especially as, by issuing its own rupees at the rate of Rs. 15 to the sovereign, " the Colony would undertake the sole burden of a liability which at present is borne by India—the liability, namely, to keep up the gold value of the rupee ". It therefore suggested increasing the supply of small silver and recommended that section 3 of Ordinance No. 13 of 1901 should be further amended so that the Currency Commissioners might have the power to decline to issue notes in exchange for gold coin whenever they thought it inexpedient to increase the amount of gold coin held as reserve. If, however, it was ruled that to refuse to issue notes for a coin which was legal tender was so opposed to sound currency principles and practice that it would be dangerous to adopt it, the Commission saw no satisfactory alternative but the repeal of Ordinance No. 13 of 1901 and also of the Order in Council constituting gold a legal tender. The Secretary of State however did not see how the Ordinance could be amended in the manner suggested by the Commission so long as the sovereign remained legal tender.

33. **Coins minted.**—The table below shows subsidiary coins minted during the period 1892–1903 inclusive :—

	Denomination.	No. of Pieces.
Silver	·50	2,700,000
	·25	5,000,000
	·10	13,500,000
Copper	·01	9,342,487
	·0¼	12,060,000

V.—1904–1936. INTRODUCTION OF NICKEL. DEMONETIZATION OF THE COPPER FIVE CENT AND QUARTER CENT PIECES AND THE SOVEREIGN. REDUCTION IN FINENESS OF SUBSIDIARY SILVER COINAGE.

34. **A nickel coinage proposed.**—In 1904 the Legislative Council raised the question whether a nickel coinage should not be substituted for the existing copper coinage. The Government of India was consulted and, as it stated that a nickel coinage for India was under consideration, the matter was put off to be taken up later. In 1907 the question was resuscitated with the introduction of the nickel anna in India, and it was proposed that, in lieu of the inconvenient and cumbersome copper five

No. 5.

Obsolete Copper Coins struck in England.

FIVE CENTS.

QUARTER CENT.

cent piece of 291·6 grs., Ceylon too should have a nickel coin of the same size and shape as the Indian anna. The proposal, however, was not approved by the Home Government owing to a strong protest by the Government of India that Ceylon should not be allowed to issue a coin resembling the Indian coins; and since it had already been decided not to adopt perforated coins for India, the Mint recommended the adoption of a square coin with rounded corners. The Secretary of State approved this recommendation.

35. **Nickel coin legalized.**—A Proclamation dated December 13, 1909 (Appendix I), declared the cupro-nickel five cent piece legal tender in Ceylon with effect from January 1, 1910. The Secretary of State for the Colonies and the Lords of the Treasury were agreed that no Order in Council was necessary for the purpose in view of section 3 of the Ceylon Coinage Order of February 6, 1892. The new coin contains 25 per cent. nickel and 75 per cent. copper and weighs 60 grains (= 3·888 grammes), the remedy allowance being a weight not exceeding the weight of one piece in every 40 pieces. A proposal to use a pure nickel coin—for the introduction of which fresh legislation was considered necessary—was abandoned on the advice, in January 1926 of Sir Thomas Rose, Chemist and Assessor of the Royal Mint.

36. **Copper five cent and quarter cent pieces demonetized.**—The Proclamation of December 13, 1909, also promulgated an Order in Council dated October 18, 1909, demonetizing the copper five cent coin as from July 1, 1910 (Appendix H). It also removed from Ceylon currency the quarter cent piece of copper with effect from the same date as it was pointed out by the Treasury that it had ceased to circulate. Although the copper five cent piece was not legal tender after June 30, 1910, an extension was allowed so that it could be exchanged for the nickel coin up to December 31, 1910, at the Treasury and the Kachcheries, and also received at Post Offices in payment for stamps, telegrams, &c.

37. **Subsidiary Silver Coinage. Millesimal fineness reduced from 800 to 550.**—When the price of silver which, in normal times, was about 29*d.* an ounce, rose to 47½*d.* in 1918, there was a great scarcity of small silver in actual circulation due to hoarding and melting, and complaints were received that it was causing much hardship in the villages. Two remedies were proposed to meet the situation: (1) to issue small currency notes as in the Straits Settlements; or (2) to mint a stock of new coins. The first proposal was dropped as it was considered that such notes would be most insanitary after a short time and very costly owing to their short life and the considerable staff that would be required in connection with their registration and destruction. The objection to the second proposal was that, if coins of the millesimal fineness of 800 prescribed by the Ceylon Coinage Order of 1892 were to be minted, the cost would exceed the face value of the coins due to the prevailing high price of silver which at the time—January 1919—had risen to 49*d.* an ounce. At this rate, it

was observed that, exclusive of freight from Calcutta to Colombo, a piece of—

·50 would cost Government	62·7 cents
·25	26·3 cents
·10	10·8 cents

whereas with silver at 29*d.* an ounce, the cost exclusive of freight, was—

37·1 cents for a	·50 piece
15·6	·25 piece
6·4	·10 piece

In these circumstances, the Government approached the Secretary of State with a view to getting the Coinage Order of 1892 amended to permit the issue of small silver with a reduced fineness of 500, which would leave a fair margin of profit, though not so large as formerly.

38. **Secretary of State agrees to a fineness of 550.**—The Secretary of State had no objection to a reduction, but did not favour the lowering of the fineness below 550. This was agreed to and an Amending Order in Council dated May 8, 1919, was issued declaring (section 1) that " 550 shall be substituted for 800 " as millesimal fineness and " 5 shall be substituted for 3 " as the corresponding remedy allowance for Ceylon fifty cent, twenty-five cent, and ten cent pieces, coined after such date as may be fixed by the Governor by Proclamation. Proclamation dated August 29, 1919, fixed September 1, 1919, as the date on which this section shall come into force (Appendix J).

39. **Demonetization of small silver coined prior to September 1, 1919, provided for.**—Section 2 of the Order in Council of 1919, further ordained that " the Governor may, by Proclamation made with the approval of the Commissioners of the Treasury and one of His Majesty's Principal Secretaries of State, declare that Ceylon fifty cent, twenty-five cent, and ten cent pieces, coined up to and including such date as may have been fixed by Proclamation under section 1 of the Order, shall cease to be legal tender notwithstanding anything in the Coinage Order, 1892, and the Orders amending that Order ".

40. **A Post-war Silver Crisis—Effects of the Indian embargo on export of silver rupees.**—In 1919 the Colombo Banks ran short of currency and experienced considerable inconvenience in financing local exports owing to the embargo on the export of silver rupees from India. This led to a serious setback in the export trade and a fall in the price of copra. The Government of India was appealed to and it granted permission to the Bank of Madras (now the Imperial Bank) to export 3 million silver rupees. The Government of Ceylon also undertook to issue to the Bank of Madras currency notes in Colombo against currency notes in Madras. The approval of the Secretary of State was obtained to invest the sum so received in currency notes in Madras in Indian 5 per cent. War Loan. Towards the end of the same year, after a Conference at Madras and discussion with the Government of India, currency notes amounting to 30 lakhs of rupees were issued to the Bank of Madras against a sterling credit in London.

41. **Lowering of legal tender rate of a sovereign in India from Rs. 15 to Rs. 10 due to rise in price of silver and exchange fluctuations.**—Since 1893 the Government of India had succeeded in maintaining the gold value of the rupee at 1*s*. 4*d*. In 1899 an Act was passed declaring the British sovereign legal tender at this rate. The price of silver rose in 1918 to 47½*d*. an ounce and in 1919 to 57*d*. Thereupon the Indian Exchange and Currency Committee recommended that the value of the rupee should be fixed at 1/10 of the gold content of a sovereign, *i.e.*, Re. 1 for 11·30016 grains of fine gold ; and in February, 1920, the Indian Government fixed a rate of 2*s*. to the rupee for the conversion of sterling into rupees and *vice versa*. By June 1920 it was found that the market rates of exchange had not only departed from the parity of gold but also, through lack of support from the export market, had fallen below the parity of 2 shillings, the price of silver having soared to 61 9/16*d*. an ounce. The Government of India therefore decided to remove as from June 21 the restrictions over import of gold bullion and coins and to declare that the sovereign and half sovereign should cease to be legal tender until further notice, but that the sovereign should be received at the existing ratio of Rs. 15 during a moratorium expiring on July 12 when it would again be legal tender at a new ratio of Rs. 10.

42. **Ceylon proposes similar action but the Secretary of State decides permanent demonetization of the sovereign in Ceylon.**—In these circumstances, the Government of Ceylon proposed to the Secretary of State in June 1920, (*a*) the further amendment of the Ceylon Coinage Amendment Order in Council of 1901, which legalized the sovereign so that sovereigns in Ceylon too should cease to be legal tender from the date of such amendment and should again be legal tender on October 1, 1920, at the new rate of Rs. 10 ; (*b*) to allow a moratorium of 14 days from the date of the further amendment of the Coinage Order during which sovereigns would be received by the Government at Rs. 15 ; and (*c*) the removal of the embargo on melting of sovereigns.* The Secretary of State had no objection to the removal of the prohibition against melting of sovereigns but preferred the entire repeal of the Coinage Amendment Order in Council of 1901, so that sovereigns might cease to be legal tender in Ceylon. He did not see sufficient reason why the Ceylon Government should give exchange of Rs. 15 to the sovereign for gold which might be left to find its own market on the basis of its intrinsic value. He was informed that, while there was no vital objection to permanent demonetization, such a course was opposed to local sentiment and would also inconvenience tourists, and it was suggested that the matter be reconsidered. He however, held that permanent demonetization was the best course and replied that the Amending Order in Council of 1901, would be repealed *in toto*. An Order in Council dated August 13, 1920, was accordingly issued directing that as from August 7 1920, sovereigns should cease to be legal tender in Ceylon (Appendix K)

* Ordinance No. 33 of 1917 empowered the Governor to prohibit the melting of gold and silver coins.

43. **Import and export of sovereigns.**—The Proclamation dated April 28, 1920, published in the *Gazette* of the 30th idem, prohibited the exportation from Ceylon of sovereigns and half-sovereigns. This prohibition was withdrawn by Proclamation dated July 30, 1920, and a general licence was issued by the Principal Collector of Customs for the importation of gold coins. When the sovereign ceased to be legal tender in Ceylon the prohibition against melting of sovereigns was withdrawn with the approval of the Secretary of State in order to encourage the flow of gold coins from the Treasury for local industrial purposes.

44. **Minting of subsidiary coins.**—With the exception of the 1912 nickel coins which came from Birmingham, the subsidiary coinage was obtained from the Royal Mint, London, until the year 1913. Thereafter, with the approval of the Secretary of State for the Colonies, the Calcutta Mint supplied small silver and copper, and the Bombay Mint the nickel coins. The latter also supplied the subsidiary silver coins of 550 fineness ordered in 1919, as the Calcutta Mint was pressed with work at the time. From 1922, all coinage was supplied by the Calcutta Mint. The change from London to Calcutta was due to considerations of cost and quicker delivery. In 1924 the Deputy Master of the Royal Mint suggested that the Ceylon coins should again be obtained from London, as the mechanical equipment and plant at the Royal Mint had been considerably extended and it was able to execute orders with greater rapidity and despatch, and was also in a position to supply the silver bullion from surplus stock at the net price of silver (*i.e.*, without the costs incurred by the Crown Agents in purchasing the metal). Accordingly, in 1926, the work was again transferred to the Royal Mint.

45. **Minting charges.**—The cost to Government in 1926 per piece of each denomination, including metal, manufacture, freight, landing charges, &c. (at Re. 1.=1*s*. 6*d*.) was—

Denomination.			Cost. Cts.
Silver	·50*	..	20·48
	·25*	..	10·64
	·10*	..	4·78
Nickel	·05	..	1·01
Copper	·01	..	·83
	·0½	..	·48

The average annual profit derived by the Government from the issue of its subsidiary coinage for the 10 years 1900–1909 amounted to Rs. 84,800.

46. **Design of Subsidiary coinage.**—The silver and copper coins now current are of the common "round" type, but the nickel piece is square with rounded corners. On the obverse the sovereign's name, title and

* Silver at 32*d*. an ounce.

No. 6.

Obsolete Copper Coins struck at the Royal Mint.

HALF STUIVER = 1/96 RD.

crowned effigy are shown facing right or left, there being a change at each accession; *e.g.* Queen Victoria faces the left, King Edward VII. the right, and King George V. the left. On the reverse, a talipot palm (except in the nickel five cent piece), the value of the coin in Sinhalese, Tamil, and English characters and in Arabic numerals (except in copper coins), the date of minting and the word "Ceylon" are impressed.

46A.* The following table giving the Sinhalese and Tamil names for various obsolete coins may be of interest, as they are still applied to various numbers of cents :—

Coin.	Name in Vernacular.	True Value in Cents.	Vulgar Value in Cents.
½ Dutch challie ..	.. *S.* Alukkala *T.* Araic-calli	25/96 ..	¼
Dutch challie (⅓ stuiver)	.. *S.* Tambasalliya *T.* Vellaic-calli, tam-paccalli	25/48 ..	½
English challie (¼ stuiver)	.. *S.* Salliya *T.* Salli	25/64 ..	½
Stuiver or pice ..	.. *S.* Tuttuwa *T.* Tuddu	1 9/16 ..	1½
Six tuttu ..	.. *S.* Sattaliya ..	9 6/16 ..	9
Fanam ..	.. *S.* Panama ..	6¼ ..	6
4 Fanams, "sixpence"	.. *S.* Panamhatara ..	25 ..	25
8 Fanams, "shilling"	.. *S.* Silima *T.* Silin	50 ..	50
Rix-dollar ..	.. *S.* Patagaya, ridi paha *T.* Iraiyal; vulgar, irasal	75 ..	75
"Pound" ..	.. *S.* Pavuma *T.* Pavun	Rs. 10 ..	Rs. 10

The fanam equals 6¼ cents, but since the introduction of the decimal system is reckoned at 6; the quarters of the rupee, however, retain their true values. Thus, 2 and 3 fanams are reckoned at 12 and 18 instead of 12½ and 18¾ cents. To reduce to cents according to the vulgar computation any number of fanams over 4, add 6 or a multiple of 6 to the value of the last quarter rupee; *e.g.*, for 6 fanams, add 12 to 25, result 37 cents, the true calculation, of course, being 37½ cents.

47. **Coins minted.**—The number of subsidiary coins minted from 1904-1929 inclusive are shown below. No coins were minted from 1930-1936.

	Denomination.		No. of Pieces.
Silver	·50	—	9,568,000
	·25	—	11,343,000
	·10	—	25,182,116
Nickel	·05	—	19,000,000
Copper	·01	—	66,847,095
	·0½	—	29,225,704

* "Ceylon Coins and Currency" by H. W. Codrington, p. 153.

48. **Circulation of subsidiary coinage.**—The estimated gross circulation of subsidiary coins at December 31, 19:4, 1924, 1934, and 1936 and the *per capita* circulation in respect of these years stood as follows :—

	Small silver.* Rs.	Nickel. Rs.	Copper. Rs.	Total. Rs.	Per capita. Rs.
1914 ..	5,907,000 ..	386,000 ..	996,305 ..	7,289,305 ..	1·74
1924 ..	10,216,211 ..	659,300 ..	1,189,705 ..	12,065,216 ..	2·51
1934 ..	9,714,961 .	700,200 ..	1,474,005 ..	11,889,166 ..	2·14
1936 ..	9,549,961 ..	730,100 ..	1,508,555 ..	11,788,616 ..	2·09

49. **Exchange.**—Ceylon having accepted the rupee of British India as her standard coin accepted also the Indian rate of exchange as her own official rate ; and when the Government of India raised it from 1*s.* 4*d.* to 2*s.* to the rupee Ceylon Government too adopted the 2*s.* rate as from October 1, 1920. When India lowered the rate to 1*s.* 4*d.* on April 1, 1923, Ceylon followed suit with effect from October 1 of the same year. The rate was again changed to 1*s.* 6*d.* with effect from October 1, 1928, and it remains the official rate of exchange to this day.

PART II.—THE PAPER CURRENCY.

VI.—1796–1883. EARLY ISSUES : KREDIT BRIEVEN, RIXDOLLAR PAPER, STERLING NOTES AND BANK NOTES.

50. **Kredit Brieven.**—**The First Paper Currency in Ceylon** was issued by the Dutch in 1785, exactly a hundred years before the establishment of the present Government Note Issue. The notes were called Kredit Brieven and were payable to bearer on demand in Ceylon copper coin at the rate of 48 stuivers for each rixdollar. The first issue was dated May 10, 1785, and consisted of notes for RD 50, 100, 500, and 1,000, to the aggregate value of RD 25,000. Each note was in Dutch, Sinhalese, and Tamil, and signed by three officials. It carried interest at 3 per cent. and had to be endorsed by the holder. The first issue was cancelled in April 1787. The second issue was in October 1785 and consisted of RD 5, 10, 20, 50, 100, 200, and 500 notes. Third and fourth issues followed in December of the same year and May 1786, and thirteen issues were made between 1787 and 1795. In addition to these, there were two issues in 1789 and 1790 for use at Batticaloa and one issue in 1788 for use at Trincomalee. In 1796 cash notes of the following denominations were also issued : RD 1, 2, 3, 4, 5, and 10. In 1793 certain Kredit Brieven were found to have been falsified and rules were made to protect the public.

51. **Kredit Brieven taken over by the British.**—In accordance with Article 6 of the Capitulation of Colombo, the British took over from the Dutch in 1796 the notes which were then in circulation up to a limit of £50,000 sterling and agreed to issue certificates for the amount bearing interest at the rate of 3 per cent. payable half-yearly.

---

* Includes ·50 and ·25 pieces issued for circulation in the Maldive Islands. The value of coins so issued in 1936 amounted to Rs. 68,000 approximately, all in fifty cent pieces. The Maldivians use these coins in addition to the silver rupee of British India and their own copper (viz., one lari and four lari pieces). 120 laris = Re. 1.

No. 7.

Front

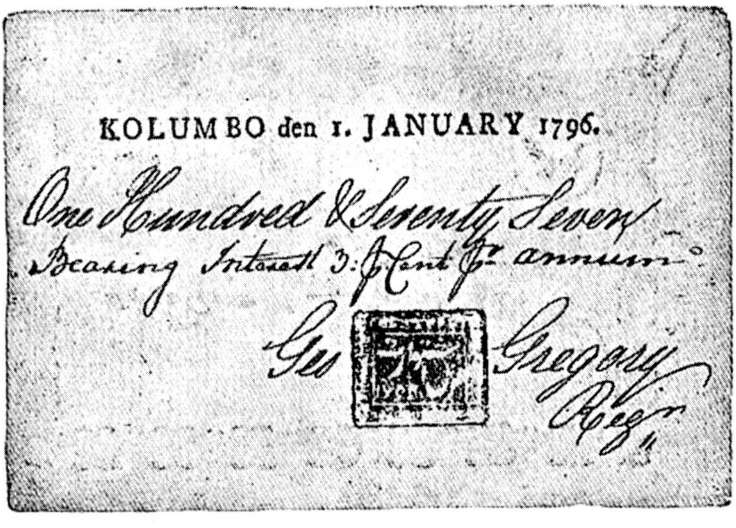

A DUTCH CASH NOTE.

Back

52. **Kredit Brieven redeemed and Rixdollar Paper issued.**—In March, 1800, currency notes, generally of the denominations of RD 100, 50, and 25, were issued by the British to the value of RD 30,000. This was followed by a second issue to the extent of RD 45,000; the Kredit Brieven being redeemed gradually*. The notes were exchangeable at the Treasury on demand at 45 fanams or RD 3¾ to the Star Pagoda. The paper commanded a small premium on account of its superior convenience to the copper money. In October 1801 the estimated note circulation was £10,000.

53. **Further Issues. Counterfeitings.**—Further issues followed and, in 1820, the paper currency amounted to nearly 2½ million rixdollars. Several counterfeits came to light and, in order to prevent forgery, Regulation 3 was issued in 1820, requiring the value of the note to be added by means of a "dry stamp". This was not found satisfactory owing to the thinness of the paper and by Regulation 7 of the same year it was replaced by a stamp in black ink on the back of the note.

54. **Withdrawal and Cancellation of Paper Rixdollars.**—By Regulation 5 of 1823 the notes of the value of RD 1 were called in as from August 31 of that year. By Regulation 8 of the same year all notes of RD 50 and 100 of a date prior to May 5 were also withdrawn, owing to a theft at the Colombo Kachcheri. Between 1820 and 1825 nearly RD 866,016 in notes had been withdrawn. The note circulation in 1825 amounted to RD 1,561,669.

55. **Sterling Notes replace Paper Rixdollars.**—When the Order in Council of March 23, 1825, introduced Sterling currency into all the Colonies, the local Government issued Regulation 8 of 1825 ordaining that public accounts should be kept in pounds, shillings, and pence. Regulation 8 of 1827 enacted that Government notes expressed in pounds payable in the currency of the Island "shall pass current at 20 shillings sterling" and a new paper currency to the extent of £90,000 was issued under this Regulation, expressed in terms of sterling money, the denominations being £ 1, 2, 5, 10, 20, 25, and 50. These notes were payable at the Treasury in specie on demand; but the holders were not allowed the right given to the holders of the old inconvertible rixdollar paper of exchanging them for bills on London at the rate fixed by the Government. By Regulation 9 of 1827 all rixdollar paper (except RD 2 and RD 5) were withdrawn and on September 1, 1830, the latter too were called in. The note circulation at that date amounted to £110,858.

56. **Privilege of Note Issue granted to Banks. Withdrawal of Sterling Notes issued by Government.**—After the close of the Napoleonic Wars, Banks began to spring up in the Colonies, the chief inducement to their establishment being the power to issue notes and the profits arising therefrom. In 1844 the local Government passed Ordinance No. 23 making it lawful for Banks, duly licensed, to issue on unstamped paper promissory notes for any sum amounting to £1 or upwards, each licence to be annual

* Most of the Kredit Brieven were purchased by Government at 60 per cent. discount. The few outstanding notes were paid off in 1912 and cancelled. *Vide* note on p. 34.

3——J. N. 81971 (2/39)

and subject to a half-yearly composition duty of 3*s*. 6*d*. for every £100 or fraction thereof, and to a stamp duty of £20 except where a Bank issued notes under the authority of a Charter or Letters Patent from the Crown. The Western Bank of India and the Bank of Ceylon (later incorporated under the title "Oriental Bank Corporation") and the Chartered Mercantile Bank of India, London, and China, issued notes under the authority of this Ordinance. On December 28, 1855, Governor Sir Henry Ward issued a Minute notifying,

> "that the whole of the Treasury Notes in circulation on January 1, 1856, will be withdrawn as they came into the hands of Government and sent to England to be cancelled; and that in order to obviate any inconvenience that might arise from the withdrawal of the Treasury Notes in commercial transactions, the notes of the Oriental Bank which by its Charter of Incorporation has given what appears to Her Majesty's Government to be a sufficient security for their convertibility will be received at all Kachcheries in payment of amounts due to the Government, precisely as the Treasury Notes have been received hitherto."

Government Notes thus ceased to exist as a medium of circulation and, after their withdrawal the notes of the Oriental Bank Corporation and the Chartered Mercantile Bank only were in circulation in the Island.

In 1861 Ordinance No. 23 of 1844 was repealed by Ordinance No. 2 which authorized the two Banks mentioned above or any other Bank authorized by Royal Charter or Letters Patent or named in any Proclamation duly issued by the Governor, to issue notes for any sum amounting to 10*s*. or upwards subject to the half-yearly payment of a composition duty of 10*s*. for every £100 or fraction thereof of the average amount of such notes issued and in circulation during such half year.

VII.—1884-1936. FAILURE OF THE ORIENTAL BANK CORPORATION AND THE RE-ESTABLISHMENT OF A STATE NOTE ISSUE.

57. **Bank suspends Payments.**—The Oriental Bank Corporation which had had a prosperous run for 33 years closed its doors on May 3, 1884, causing a collapse of credit and bringing the trade of the Island to a standstill. Its note issue at the time amounted to Rs. 3,211,085. The note issue of the Chartered Mercantile Bank, the only other bank which issued notes, amounted to Rs. 921,495. The notes of the Oriental Bank therefore formed an integral part of the Island's currency, and when these suddenly lost their value the panic among all classes of the community was immediate and severe. Taxes could not be collected, Courts of Justice approached, labour employed, nor even provisions bought without considerable difficulty. It was even found necessary to suspend for 24 hours the payment of Post Office orders.

58. **Governor guarantees Bank Notes and recommends a Government Note Issue.**—Sir Arthur Gordon, with statesmanlike courage and promptitude intervened and in order to arrest the growing panic and restore

No. 8.

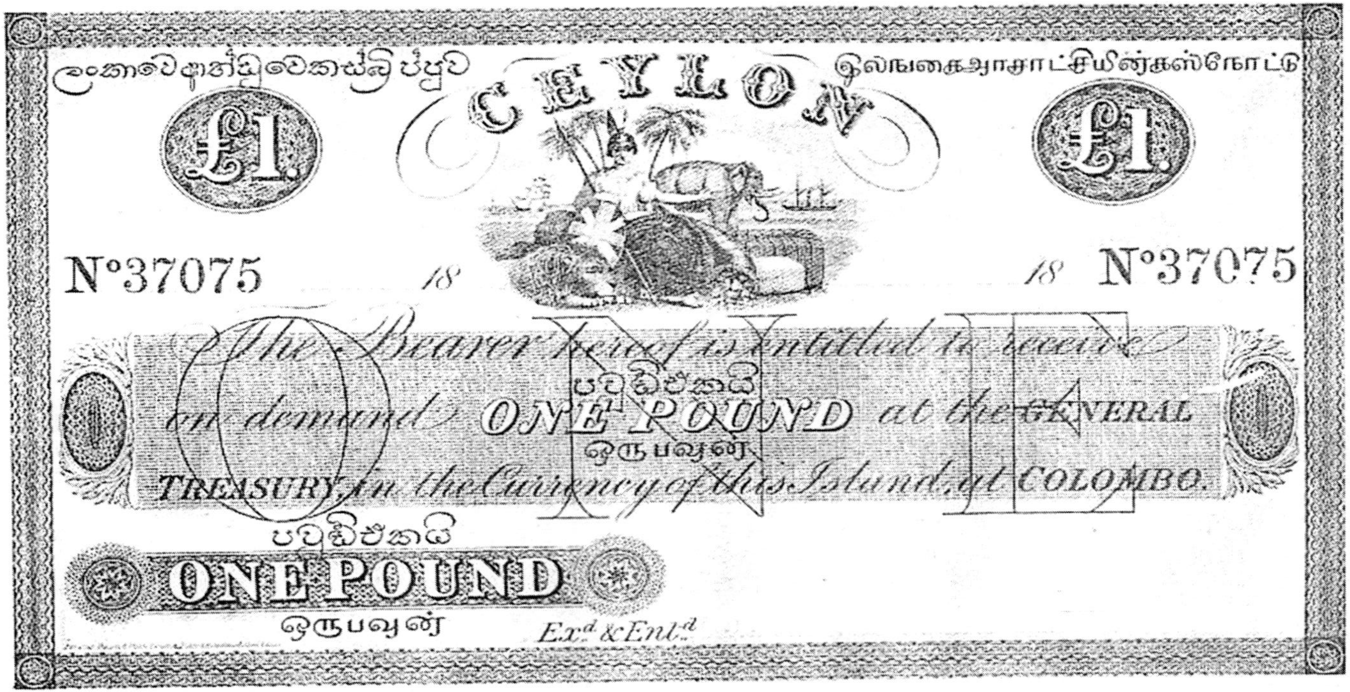

A STERLING NOTE.

confidence, undertook on May 5, 1884, to transfer to the Colonial Exchequer the obligations of the insolvent bank in respect of the notes then in circulation in the Island. In informing the Secretary of State of the undertaking given, the Governor requested him not to concede the privilege of a note issue to any bank that may be about to replace the Oriental Bank, and proposed the establishment of a Government Note Issue, submitting a draft ordinance and urging, *inter alia*, as follows :—

"The Oriental Bank Corporation has enjoyed the privilege of a note issue in Ceylon ; it has had the advantage of a very large portion of the banking business of the local Government ; every provision that ingenuity could devise to secure its stability was included in its Charter and imposed on it by law ; yet on the 3rd instant it suspended payment with disastrous consequences. What has happened in the case of this bank, may, and probably will, happen again in the case of any bank that may take its place with the privilege of a note issue. We shall again see the paper currency of the country depreciate in a day 50 per cent. within a stone's throw of the bank itself, and rendered wholly valueless in more distant places ; we shall again see a universal dislocation of all business and a total collapse of credit, including that of the Government itself, threatened.

"We shall again be brought face to face with the fact, on the one hand of the people being unable to buy food and, on the other, with that of the chetties who are the principal rice dealers in the country trooping to the Solicitor-General for leave to use fire arms in the defence of their stores ; and again will Government inevitably be compelled to intervene with a guarantee,—fortunate if by such intervention, it may avert at the risk of heavy pecuniary loss still graver disaster and calamity.

"Is it wise, is it right, is it possible, willingly to invite a repetition of such events ? Is it worthwhile to incur such perils for the sake of adherence,—I am inclined to say a pedantic adherence—to general rules laid down some 30 years ago, under conditions wholly different and with a view to circumstances altogether dissimilar ? These dangers will be risked, and the scenes of last week in all human probability be repeated, if the privilege of a note issue be granted to the successor of the Oriental Bank. They will certainly be avoided, so long as Ceylon remains a Crown Colony, if the note issue be undertaken by the Government."

59. **Home Authorities take exception to Guarantee.**—The Secretary of State (Lord Derby) and the Lords of the Treasury, while being deeply impressed with the difficulties of the situation, however, took exception to the guarantee given, the latter observing,—

(*a*) that the Governor should have first telegraphed to the Secretary of State full details of his situation with a request for instructions ;

(b) that he should have considered the possibility of effecting a combination among the leading residents of Colombo and merchants for the guarantee of the notes which he assumed himself* ; and

(c) that steps might have been taken to obtain the use of the silver reserve in the bank's vault by an arrangement with the representative of the bank made without prejudice to the ultimate right of creditors, pending the arrival of specie from India.

They also pointed out that the issue to be decided was one of those which by the Royal Instructions and by special Circular Despatch of August 18, 1875, have been expressly reserved for the decision of the Home Government upon whom the responsibility ultimately rests whatever course of action be taken on the spot by the Governor.

Nevertheless, while the Secretary of State was disposed to think that in some details the measure might perhaps have been differently treated, he was not prepared to censure the Governor for the decision he took in the face of a crushing disaster, the full nature and gravity of which it was difficult to appreciate correctly at such a great distance from the scene of action.

60. **Councils support the Governor.**—Both the Legislative and Executive Councils, however, strongly supported the Governor, the former presenting an Address of Appreciation, and the latter submitting a memorandum to the Home Government explaining that any attempt to act as was suggested by the Lords Commissioners of the Treasury would have rendered the Government practically bankrupt, a result which must inevitably have followed in any case but for the guarantee which, by maintaining confidence and giving currency to the notes of the Oriental Bank, had the effect, among others, of averting it. It was further pointed out that the notes of the Oriental Bank had been virtually guaranteed by the local Government at an earlier period, the reference being to Sir Henry Ward's Minute of December 28, 1855 (paragraph 56, *supra*).

61. **Governor's Explanation.**—Sir Arthur Gordon's reply may best be stated in his own words :—

"It is not my intention to offer any reply to the observations of the Lords of the Treasury beyond the remark which I think it due to myself to make, that I do not admit either their justice or their accuracy; and that they very plainly show that their Lordships are in great measure unaware of the facts of the position in which the Colony was placed on the 3rd of May, and fail to realize what position it would now occupy had the guarantee not been given. That this should be the case is very probably in a great degree my own fault, in having failed to describe with sufficient strength and vividness the actual state of affairs.

* In the Straits Settlements where the Colonial Government abstained from following the Ceylon precedent, the other Banks in self-defence took on themselves the onus of cashing the Oriental Bank's notes in local circulation. "History of Currency in the British Colonies" by Robert Chalmers, p. 36.

I have not much leisure for careful writing, and it is quite possible that I have been too far influenced by my reluctance to paint highly coloured and sensational pictures.

"Knowing myself what I do know of the danger incurred I am still fully convinced that had the guarantee not been given calamities would have ensued, the effects of which would have been long and disastrously felt by the Colony, and which it was my duty to avert even at the risk of misconception and censure."

62. **Lords Commissioners of the Treasury approve Government Note Issue.**—Neither Downing street nor Treasury Chambers made any further adverse comments regarding the guarantee. The Lords Commissioners of the Treasury were, however, not quite satisfied with the position of affairs. But in view of the exceptional circumstances of the case and the peculiar situation created by the guarantee, they gave their assent to the establishment of a Government Note Issue on the model of that already existing in Mauritius, after pointing out to Lord Derby that they did not think that the failure of a bank in Ceylon, and the natural but perhaps exaggerated alarm of a Governor not specially versed in economic subjects, justified a reversal of a policy founded on approved authority*. Arrangements were made to cancel the powers of note issue granted to the Chartered Mercantile Bank by the existing Charter when it came up for renewal on its expiration in 1888; and the Governor was empowered to introduce the necessary legislation to give effect to the proposals as amended by the Commissioners of the Treasury.

63. **Law Regulating the Government Note Issue.**—The present Government Note Issue is regulated by Ordinance No. 32 of 1884 (cited as the principal Ordinance), as amended by Ordinances Nos. 12 of 1886, 13 of 1901, 6 of 1903, 11 of 1909, 33 of 1914, and 1 of 1917 (Appendix L). Important sections of the principal Ordinance and subsequent amendments are summarized below.

(*a*) **Board of Currency Commissioners created.**—Section 3 establishes a Board consisting of the Colonial Secretary, the Treasurer, and the Auditor-General.

Amending Ordinance 12 of 1886 creates the Board of Currency Commissioners a "corporation" with continuance for ever, under the name and style of "The Ceylon Currency Commissioners" (*a*) with full power and authority to have and use a common seal, the said seal to be fixed to any instrument in the presence of at least one of the commissioners and (*b*) with power to appoint officers or agents for recovering dividends, interest, &c. This amendment became necessary as under section 15 of the principal Ordinance all investments in

* The Imperial Government had traditionally preferred private issues and never favoured the issue of Notes by Colonial Governments and, until 1884, Mauritius afforded the only example of a State Issue in Crown Colonies.—"History of Currency in the British Colonies" by Robert Chalmers.

Indian Government Securities had to be made in the *names* of the Commissioners and each time there happened to be a change in the *personnel* of the Commissioners, a fresh power of attorney was required to authorize an Agent in India to collect interest. There was also a serious omission in section 18 : it enacted that dividends, &c., should be paid to such person as shall be nominated, but did not say by whom such person should be nominated.

Gazette notification dated July 6, 1931, substituted the Financial Secretary for the Colonial Secretary the Deputy Chief Secretary for the Treasurer and the Commissioner of Stamps* for the Auditor-General.

(*b*) **Commissioners to issue Government Promissory Notes.**—Sections 4–6 as amended by Ordinance No. 13 of 1901 empower the Commissioners to issue currency notes payable to bearer on demand at the office of the Commissioners in Colombo for the respective sums of 5, 10, 50, 100, 500, and 1,000 rupees in exchange for silver rupees of India or gold coin which is legal tender in Ceylon but no other coin ; every such note is to bear the signatures or facsimiles of the signatures of any two of the Commissioners holding office at the date borne on the note.

Amending Ordinance No. 1 of 1917 gives the Commissioners the power to treat a credit at the Bank of England as equivalent to a deposit of gold. It also empowers them to issue one-rupee and two-rupee notes.

(*c*) **Notes legal tender.**—Section 7 makes every currency note legal tender for the amount expressed thereon.

Amending Ordinance No. 1 of 1917 makes every currency note legal tender in Ceylon for the payment of any amount.

(*d*) **Exchange of Oriental Bank Notes for Government Notes.**—Sections 8 to 10 : After 31st March, 1885, the Bank's note issue in circulation on May 3, 1884, shall cease to be recognized as equivalent to money by the Government ; and after February 15, 1885, and until March 31, 1885, the Commissioners shall issue currency notes in exchange for bank notes, provided they were in circulation on May 3, 1884. The said notes shall be deposited in the Treasury.

(*e*) **Issue of currency notes in exchange for gold coin** legally current is authorized except when it appears inexpedient to the Commissioners to increase the amount of gold coins held as reserve—section 11 as amended by Ordinance No. 6 of 1903.

(In 1920 the gold coins were taken out of the reserve, when they ceased to be legal tender as from August 7. *Vide* Proclamation in *Gazette* No. 7,121 of August 7, 1920.)

---

* Notification dated January 17, 1939, substituted the Deputy Financial Secretary for the Commissioner of Stamps.

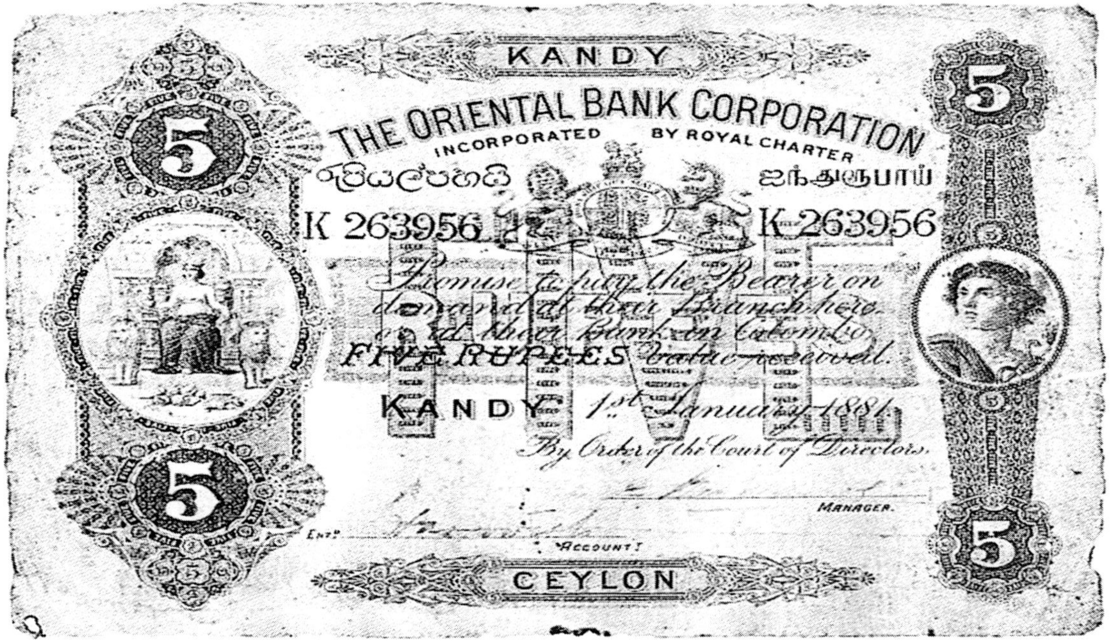

No. 9. AN ORIENTAL BANK NOTE.

(*f*) **Currency Reserve.**—Sections 12–14 as amended by Ordinance No. 13 of 1901 : Commissioners are empowered to retain a reserve in silver rupees or in gold coin of one half of the amount of currency notes in circulation—section 12 ; and to invest the other half in Indian Government and United Kingdom or Colonial except Ceylon) Government Securities, provided that not more than one-half of such sum shall be in Indian Government securities except by sanction of the Secretary of State—section 13. The reserve in coin and securities is to be set apart to satisfy notes—section 14.

(At one stage, the metallic portion of the reserve included subsidiary coins. These were taken off the reserve in 1916.)

(*g*) **Sale or Exchange of Investments.**—Sections 15–16 : The Crown Agents along with a nominee of His Majesty's Secretary of State for the Colonies are appointed as trustees in respect of investments made in England. The Indian securities are to be in the names of the Commissioners. Power is given to both to sell or exchange investments as directed by the Governor. Securities are to be sold, if the specie reserve falls below one-third of the value of the notes in circulation ; and no further investment is to be made until that reserve shall amount to one-half at the least of the amount of notes in circulation—section 17.

Amending Ordinance No. 1 of 1917 suspends the operation of the above requirements as from December 30, 1916, and also the limit of the proportion of the value of notes in circulation which may be invested in securities under section 13 of the principal Ordinance. (This was done as a war measure but the suspension still stands.)

(*h*) **Revenue from securities.**—Section 18 : Dividends, interest, and other revenue from investments shall be credited to general revenue, excepting 1 per cent. which shall be appropriated annually on the whole amount of such investments, to be separately invested and to form part of the reserve set apart to satisfy notes. The Governor may with the Secretary of State's sanction order the discontinuance of such appropriation at any time wholly or partially.

In 1896 the Secretary of State sanctioned the discontinuance of the 1 per cent. appropriation until such time as the market value of "Reserve and Depreciation Fund" securities together falls below 110 per cent. of the cost price of "Reserve" securities alone. Amending Ordinance No. 11 of 1909 abolished the "Depreciation Fund" and authorized the transfer of the proceeds to "Reserve Fund" ; but laid down that account should not be taken of the amount of such proceeds in computing the investments under section 13 of the principal Ordinance.

(*i*) **Accounts** showing profits, expenses, &c., shall be published annually in *Government Gazette*—section 19 : and an abstract showing notes in circulation, reserve. nominal value, as well as the latest known market value, and the cost price of the securities shall be prepared on the 10th day of each month and published as soon as may be in the *Gazette*—section 20.

(*j*) **Maximum Penalty.**—20 years' imprisonment for counterfeiting notes—section 21; 5 years' for possession of counterfeited or incomplete notes—section 22; and 5 years' for possession of paper, moulds, &c., for manufacture of notes—section 23.

Amending Ordinance No. 33 of 1914 provides for the issue of a certificate under the hand of the Treasurer (now Deputy Financial Secretary) which would be conclusive evidence in any Court of law as to the spuriousness of a currency note.

64. **Note Circulation.**—The Ceylon Government currency notes were brought into circulation in January, 1885, notes of the denominations of Rs. 5, Rs. 10, and Rs. 50 being the first to be issued. The Rs. 100 note followed in October. The Rs. 1,000 note was issued in August, 1899; the one-rupee note and the two-rupee note in May, 1917, as a war measure; and the Rs. 500 note in April, 1927. Booklets containing 25 one-rupee notes, 25 two-rupee notes and 20 five-rupee notes were introduced in 1923, 1927, and 1930, respectively. The Rs. 500 note has a very small circulation. The one-rupee note has become so popular that it has driven out of circulation almost entirely the silver rupee, the standard coin of the Island. At the end of the first year of issue the note circulation (gross) amounted to Rs. 4,192,165. At December 31, 1888, it stood at Rs. 5,529,705. Its steady rise since then and its decline after the great depression will be seen from the table below which shows also the position of the currency reserve.

Date.	Gross Circulation.	Reserve.	
		Metallic.	Securities at cost.
	Rs.*	Rs.*	Rs.*
1. 10. 1898	11,278	5,665	5,613
1. 10. 1908	15,007	6,371	8,636
1. 10. 1918	37,340	18,029	19,311
1. 10. 1928	57,436	22,509	42,477
1. 10. 1936	44,334	14,158	36,137

* 000 omitted.

The note circulation reached its "peak" level in 1926 when it stood at Rs. 62,868,615 on November 5. The "per capita" circulation which stood at Re. 1·77 in 1886 steadily rose to Rs. 10·68 in 1920. It fell to Rs. 8·55 in 1923, shot up to Rs. 12·23 in 1926 (the highest figure on record), and declined to Rs. 7·76 in 1933. It stood at Rs. 7·87 in 1936.

65. **Currency Reserve and Profits.**—At September 30, 1936, the proportion of the metallic reserve to the note circulation was 31·93 per cent; and the market value of securities amounted to Rs. 42,482,000. The currency profits for the 7 years ending September 30, 1936, amounted to

Rs. 11,199,701, or an annual average of Rs. 1,599,957. In the 7 years ending December 31, 1891, the profits amounted to Rs. 467,878 or Rs. 66,839 per annum on an average.

66. **Design of Currency Notes.**—The notes of the denominations of Rs. 2 and over are printed on watermarked mould-made paper. They bear the facsimiles of the signatures of two of the Commissioners and serial numbers with a prefix letter over a prefix number thus: $\frac{P}{90}$ 25657. Notes of the earliest issue bore no facsimile signatures but were signed at time of issue. The watermarks are as follows :—

Rs.	Left	Centre	Right
2	..Dagoba .. Elephant..	TWO RUPEES GOVERNMENT OF CEYLON	..Dagoba ..Elephant
5	do. ..	5 CEYLON	.. do.
10	.. do. ..	10 CEYLON	.. do.
50	..Dagoba .. Elephant .. Flower ..	FIFTY RUPEES GOVERNMENT OF CEYLON	..3 long and 1 short wave lines
100	.. do. ..	ONE HUNDRED RUPEES GOVERNMENT OF CEYLON	.. do.
500	.. do. ..	FIVE HUNDRED RUPEES GOVERNMENT OF CEYLON	.. do.
1000	.. do. ..	ONE THOUSAND RUPEES GOVERNMENT OF CEYLON	.. do.

The size of notes differs according to denominations as indicated below.

Rs.	Inches		Inches
1	$4\frac{1}{2} \times 2\frac{1}{2}$		—
2	5×3		—
5	$6\frac{3}{4} \times 5\frac{1}{4}$	reduced in 1930 to	$5\frac{1}{2} \times 3\frac{1}{2}$
10	$7\frac{3}{4} \times 5$	do.	6×4
50	$9\frac{1}{4} \times 5$	do.	$6\frac{1}{2} \times 4\frac{1}{2}$
100	$8\frac{1}{2} \times 5\frac{5}{8}$	—	—
500	$9\frac{3}{16} \times 6$	—	—
1000	$9\frac{1}{4} \times 5\frac{3}{4}$	reduced in 1930 to	8×6

In order to afford greater security against counterfeiting a multi-colour protection rainbow tint was added to Rs. 5 and Rs. 10 notes as from 1925, and to Rs. 50 and Rs. 1,000 notes as from 1930. A design was also printed on the back of the one-rupee note in blue; Rs. 2, Rs. 5, and Rs. 50 notes in green ; Rs. 10 note in mauve, and Rs. 1,000 note in brown. In the earlier issues the serial number appears only on the two top corners of the notes. In later issues the number is printed on the four corners, except in the case of the Re. 1 note where the number appears on the left bottom and right top corners only. As a further mark of difference to catch the eye the number is printed in black on the one-rupee note ; in dark green on the Rs. 2 note ; in red on the Rs. 5 note, Rs. 500 note and the Rs. 1,000 note ; in blue on the Rs. 10 note ; and in dark red on the Rs. 50 note and the Rs. 100 note.

Note—vide *para 52.*

The Dutch promissory notes taken over by the British Government in 1796, were never called in. The question of their redemption came up for consideration during Sir Robert Peel's ministry when an application was received in 1846, from a holder in England for the payment of the face value (28,123 rixdollars) in sterling (£2,109.4.6.) in respect of 237 Kredit Brieven and 120 cash notes for which he was receiving annually £61.7.6¾. as interest at the rate of 3 per cent. per annum less 3 per cent. premium due to the Ceylon Government in consequence of the payment being made in England. Mr. W. E. Gladstone then expressed the opinion that it was obvious from the terms of the Capitulation that the holders of the certificates given in lieu of the promissory notes of the Dutch Government were not entitled to demand their redemption by the Government and that Her Majesty's Government could not sanction a compliance with the application.

The Government found that the promissory notes had depreciated in value by 50 per cent. to 60 per cent., and published a notification dated January 24, 1857, in the *Gazette* of the same date giving notice that the holders of the Dutch Kredit Brieven and cash notes, on presenting same at the Treasury, Colombo, would be paid at the rate of £40 for every £100 of nominal principal. Thereafter most of the notes were purchased by Government at 60 per cent. discount and cancelled.

In 1894 negotiations were started with a view to paying off the 357 notes amounting to 28,123 rixdollars, the Government offerring the holder 75 per cent. of their value in rupees (at 75 cents a rixdollar) converted into sterling at 1*s.* 2*d.*, current rate of exchange ; but the holder was not prepared to accept anything less than the sterling value at 1*s.* 6*d.* a rixdollar as originally fixed. In 1896 however on the death of the holder his heir accepted an offer of £1,250 plus an annuity of £25 for life and surrendered the notes.

There were still outstanding 122 Kredit Brieven and 8 cash notes amounting to 18,887 rixdollars with four holders in Ceylon on which a sum of Rs. 425 was being paid annually as interest out of the Public Debt vote and, in 1907, the Treasurer proposed that these notes too should be paid off. The Attorney-General (Sir Anton Bertram) whilst stating that it was with the greatest diffidence that one ventured to differ from such an authority as Mr. Gladstone thought that it was possible that he did not minutely scrutinize the terms of the Capitulation, and expressed the opinion (the Solicitor-General concurring) that the liability to pay interest carried with it a corresponding right to discharge that liability and that the Government might pay off the notes at the face value. After obtaining the approval of the Secretary of State and protracted negotiations with the holders the Government bought in the 130 notes in 1912, for a sum of Rs. 13,890 and cancelled them, thus wiping off finally a permanent charge on public funds.

APPENDICES.

APPENDIX A.

Order in Council of 23rd March, 1825.

WHEREAS it has been represented to His Majesty at this Board, by the Lords Commissioners of His Majesty's Treasury, that they have given directions that His Majesty's troops serving in the several British colonies and possessions abroad should, in certain cases, be paid in British silver and copper money; and that, with a view of securing the circulation of such money in those colonies, it would be expedient that an Order in Council should be issued declaring that in all those colonies where the Spanish dollar is now, either by law, fact, or practice, considered as a legal tender for the discharge of debts, or where the duties to the Government are rated or collected, or the individuals have a right to pay, in that description of coin, that a tender and payment of British silver money to the amount of 4*s*. 4*d*. should be considered as equivalent to the tender or payment of one Spanish dollar, and so in proportion for any greater or less amount of debt:

And whereas it has been further represented by the Lords Commissioners of His Majesty's Treasury that, with respect to the Cape of Good Hope, where there are not any Spanish dollars in circulation, but where the circulation consists entirely of paper rixdollars and its proportions, and with respect to **Ceylon,** where the circulation consists of silver and paper rixdollars, as well as of a variety of other coins which are generally received and paid with relation to their value as compared with rixdollars, it would be expedient that a tender and payment of 1*s*. 6*d*. in British silver money should be considered as equivalent to a tender and payment of one such rixdollar so current at the Cape of Good Hope and **Ceylon** respectively, and so in proportion for any greater or less sum; and also that British copper should be made a legal tender in all the British colonies, for its due and proper proportions of British silver money, as by law established in Great Britain, but that no person should be compelled to take more than 12*d*. in copper money at any one payment:

His Majesty, having taken the said representation into consideration, is pleased, by and with the advice of His Privy Council, to approve of what is therein proposed; and the Right Honourable the Lords Commissioners of His Majesty's Treasury, and the Right Honourable Earl Bathurst, one of His Majesty's Principal Secretaries of State, are to give the necessary directions herein, as to them may respectively appertain.

APPENDIX B.

Order in Council of 16th October, 1852.

WHEREAS there was this day read at the Board the draft of a Proclamation regulating the currency of the coins of the United Kingdom in Her Majesty's colonies in Australia, New Zealand, **Ceylon,** Mauritius, and Hong Kong:

Her Majesty, having taken the same into consideration, was pleased, by and with the advice of Her Privy Council, to approve thereof, and to order, and it is hereby ordered that the said Proclamation do take effect and come into force in Her Majesty's said colonies, or any of them, from and after the date of the publication thereof by the Governor, Lieutenant-Governor, or other Officer Administering the Government of the same respectively.

And the Lords Commissioners of Her Majesty's Treasury, and the Right Honourable Sir John Pakington, Bart., one of Her Majesty's Principal Secretaries of State, are to give the requisite directions herein accordingly.

PROCLAMATION BY THE QUEEN.

WHEREAS it has been represented to Us that in Our colonies in Australia, New Zealand, **Ceylon**, Mauritius, and Hong Kong the silver coins of Our United Kingdom pass current as an unlimited tender for payments and it is expedient that the regulations which govern the circulation of the coins of Our United Kingdom, as by law established, should be enforced in Our said colonies:

Now therefore We, by the advice of Our Privy Council, have thought fit to declare and ordain, and by the advice aforesaid We do hereby declare and ordain, that within and throughout Our colonies in Australia, New Zealand, **Ceylon**, Mauritius, and Hong Kong the coins of Our United Kingdom shall pass current in the manner directed in the several Acts of Parliament which regulate the currency of the same, and that the silver coins of Our United Kingdom shall not be a legal tender in payment of sums exceeding forty shillings.

Order in Council of 22nd October, 1856.

HIS EXCELLENCY THE GOVERNOR, with the advice of the Executive Council, has been pleased to direct that the following Order of Her Majesty in Council, passed on the 22nd October, 1856, to legalize the currency of Australian Sovereigns and Half Sovereigns in Ceylon and elsewhere, be published for general information.

By His Excellency's command,

Colonial Secretary's Office,
Colombo, July 15, 1857.

C. J. MACCARTHY,
Colonial Secretary.

At the Court at Windsor, the 22nd day of October, 1856.

Present:

THE QUEEN'S MOST EXCELLENT MAJESTY.
HIS ROYAL HIGHNESS PRINCE ALBERT.

Viscount Palmerston, Mr. Labouchere,
Lord Stanley of Alderley, Sir George Grey, Bt.

WHEREAS there was this day read at the Board, the Draft of a Proclamation declaring the rates at which certain Gold Coins to be called Australian Sovereigns and Half Sovereigns which have been and are intended to be struck at Her Majesty's Branch of the Royal Mint at Sydney in New South Wales are to pass current in Her Majesty's Colonies of *Ceylon*, Mauritius, and Hong Kong · Her Majesty having taken the same into consideration, was pleased by and with the advice of Her Privy Council to approve thereof, and to Order, and it is hereby ordered, that the said Proclamation (copy whereof is hereunto annexed) do take effect and come into force in each of Her Majesty's said Colonies and Possessions, upon and from and after the promulgation thereof, by the Governors, or Officers Administering the Government of the said Colonies, respectively. And the Lords Commissioners of Her Majesty's Treasury, and the Right Honourable Henry Labouchere, one of Her Majesty's principal Secretaries of State, are to give the necessary directions therein accordingly.

WM. L. BATHURST.

VICTORIA R.

WHEREAS by an Order in Council, bearing date the 19th day of August, 1853, We have thought fit to order that a Branch of Our Royal Mint, should be established at or near Sydney in New South Wales.

And whereas in the 18th year of Our Reign, by an Order in Council, dated the 18th day of October, 1854, We have thought fit to order that certain pieces of Gold Money should be coined at the said Branch of Our Royal Mint, to be called respectively Australian Sovereigns, and Australian Half Sovereigns, and to be of the same respective weights, fineness, and values, with the Sovereigns, and Half Sovereigns, now current within this Our Realm.

And whereas, pursuant to and in virtue of the powers given in Our said Orders in Council, it is provided, that a coinage of the said Australian Sovereigns, and Half Sovereigns shall be made, and that every such Australian Sovereign, shall have for the obverse the Effigy of Her Majesty, with the Inscription " Victoria D. G. Britanniar : Regina F. D. " and the date of the year, and for the Reverse the word " Australia ", placed in the centre of the piece, encircled by a Laurel Wreath, and surmounted by the Royal Crown, with the Inscription " Sydney Mint, One Sovereign", and with a graining on the edge and that every such Australian Half Sovereign, shall have the obverse in every respect similar to that of the Sovereign, and for the Reverse the same word " Australia " in the centre, encircled and surmounted in like manner, but for the Inscription the words " Sydney Mint, Half Sovereign", and a graining on the Edge.

And whereas pieces of Gold Money have been and will be coined at Our said Branch of the Royal Mint in pursuance of Orders issued and to be issued, We therefore by and with the advice of Our Privy Council, have thought fit to issue this Our Royal Proclamation, and We do Ordain, Declare, and Command, that the said pieces of Gold money so to be coined shall be current and lawful money within Our Colonies of *Ceylon*, Mauritius, and Hong Kong, and shall pass and be received as current and lawful money therein by the names aforesaid, and at the values hereinbefore assigned to them.

Given at Our Court at Windsor, this Twenty-second day of October, in the Year of Our Lord One thousand Eight hundred and Fifty-six, and in the Twentieth of Our Reign.

GOD SAVE THE QUEEN.

(The *Ceylon Government Gazette* No. 3,044 of July 25, 1857.)

APPENDIX C.

VICTORIA, by the Grace of GOD, of the United Kingdom of Great Britain and Ireland, Queen, Defender of the Faith.

PROCLAMATION.

By His Excellency SIR HERCULES GEORGE ROBERT ROBINSON, Knight Commander of the Most Distinguished Order of Saint Michael and Saint George, Governor and Commander-in-Chief in and over the Island of Ceylon, with the Dependencies thereof.

HERCULES ROBINSON.

WHEREAS We have received from the Right Honourable the Secretary of State for the Colonies Her Majesty's Order in Council and Proclamation, as follows :—

At the Court of Windsor, the 18th day of June, 1869.

Present :

THE QUEEN'S MOST EXCELLENT MAJESTY
in Council,

WHEREAS there was this day read at the Board the Draft of a Proclamation for the regulation of the currency of Her Majesty's Colony of Ceylon (copy whereof is hereunto annexed), and Her Majesty having taken the same into consideration, was pleased, by and with the advice of Her Privy Council, to approve thereof, and to order, and it is hereby ordered, that the said Proclamation do take effect and come into force in Her Majesty's Colony of Ceylon in the manner thereby directed,

And the Lords Commissioners of Her Majesty's Treasury, and the Right Honourable Earl Granville, one of Her Majesty's Principal Secretaries of State, are to give the necessary directions herein accordingly.

ARTHUR HELPS.

DRAFT PROCLAMATION.

1. WHEREAS by an Order in Council, bearing date 23rd March, 1825, We were pleased, by and with the advice of Our Privy Council, to declare that a tender and payment of 1*s.* 6*d.* in British Silver money should be considered as equivalent to a tender and payment of one Rixdollar current at the Cape of Good Hope and at Ceylon, and so in proportion of any greater or less sum, and also that British Copper money should be made a legal tender in all the British Colonies, as by law established in Great Britain :

2. And whereas by an Order in Council, bearing date 16th October, 1852, We were pleased, by and with the advice of Our Privy Council, to approve of the Draft of a Proclamation declaring that in and throughout Our Colonies in Australia, New Zealand, Ceylon, Mauritius, and Hong Kong, the coins of the United Kingdom shall pass current in the manner directed in the several Acts of Parliament which regulate the currency of the said Island that the Silver coins of the United Kingdom shall not be a legal tender in payment of sums exceeding forty shillings :

3. And whereas by an Order in Council, bearing date the 22nd October, 1856, We were pleased, by and with the advice of Our Privy Council, to approve of the Draft of a Proclamation declaring the rates at which

Australian Sovereigns and Half Sovereigns coined at the Branch of Our Royal Mint at Sydney in New South Wales are to pass current in Our Colonies of Ceylon, Mauritius, and Hong Kong:

4. Now We, by the advice of Our Privy Council, have thought fit to declare and ordain, and by the advice aforesaid, We do hereby declare and ordain, that from and after a day to be fixed by the Governor or Officer Administering the Government of Ceylon, by Proclamation, the said hereinbefore recited Order in Council of 23rd March, 1825, and so much of the Orders in Council and Proclamations of the 16th October, 1852, and the 22nd October, 1856, respectively, as have effect and are in force in the Colony of Ceylon, shall be revoked and annulled.

5. And We do hereby further ordain and declare, that from and after the same date the Regulations of the Ceylon Government No. 8 of 1825 and No. 8 of 1827, entitled respectively :—

"A Regulation for declaring the legal and established Currency of the Island of Ceylon to be the Silver and Copper current coin of Great Britain, and also the Ceylon Silver and Paper Rixdollar and the Copper sub-divisions thereof already current therein."

And,

"A Regulation for declaring that all Government Notes expressed in Pounds shall be received and taken at the value expressed in the same."

shall be repealed.

6. And We do hereby further ordain and declare, that from and after the same date, (and subject to further directions to be given by Proclamation of the Governor), the British and local Copper or Bronze coins or tokens at present in circulation in Our Colony of Ceylon and its Dependencies, and such other copper or bronze tokens as may from time to time be specified by the Governor by Proclamation, shall be a legal tender of payment for any sum not exceeding half a Rupee ; the said British and local tokens to continue current until the date of such Proclamation, at the same rates as regards the Rupee as those at which they at present pass by long-established usage and custom, viz. :—

The Penny at the rate of	$\frac{2}{3}$rds of an Anna, or		8 Pie.
The Half-penny	,,	$\frac{1}{3}$rd	,,	4 ,,
The Farthing	,,	$\frac{1}{6}$th	,,	2 ,,
The Ceylon Fanam	,,	1	Anna.	
,, Stiver or Pice	,,	$\frac{1}{4}$th of an Anna, or		3 ,,
,, Challie	,,	1/12th	,,	1 ,,

7. And We do hereby further declare and ordain, that from and after the same date the silver Company's Rupee of India of 180 grains' weight, and 11th–12th fineness, as now legally current in India, and its silver subdivisions of proportionate intrinsic value, consisting of the half rupee (8 annas), the quarter rupee (4 annas), and the eighth of a rupee (2 annas), shall be the only legal tender of payment (except as hereinbefore directed) within Our Colony of Ceylon and its Dependencies.

8. And We do hereby further ordain and declare, that whenever the denomination of British Currency shall have been specified in any Regulation, Ordinance, Proclamation, Minute, Notification, or Contract in force at the date as aforesaid of the bringing into operation of this Proclamation whether as payments to be made to or by the Ceylon Government, such

sums shall continue as heretofore to be received at and paid from the local Treasuries of the Island in Rupees, and the legal subordinate currency of the Colony at the rate of Two Shillings to the Rupee.

9. And we do hereby further declare and ordain that all other contracts and engagements expressed in terms of British money, in force at the same date and payable in Our Colony, shall be defrayable in Rupees at the above rate, unless such contract or engagement shall contain any special provision or agreement to the contrary.

Now therefore, We, the said Governor of Ceylon, in pursuance and exercise of the authority vested in Us by the said Order in Council and Proclamation, do hereby proclaim and direct that the said Proclamation shall and do take effect and come into force in Her Majesty's Colony of Ceylon and the Dependencies thereof, from and after the First day of January, 1872.

Given at Colombo, in the said Island of Ceylon, this Twenty-third day of August, in the year of Our Lord One thousand Eight hundred and Seventy-one.

By His Excellency's command,

CHARLES P. LAYARD,
Acting Colonial Secretary.

GOD SAVE THE QUEEN.

(The *Ceylon Government Gazette* No. 3,836 of August 26, 1871.)

APPENDIX D.

VICTORIA, by the Grace of GOD, of the United Kingdom of Great Britain and Ireland, Queen, Defender of the Faith.

PROCLAMATION.

By His Excellency Sir HERCULES GEORGE ROBERT ROBINSON, Knight Commander of the Most Distinguished Order of Saint Michael and Saint George, Governor and Commander-in-Chief in and over the Island of Ceylon, with the Dependencies thereof.

HERCULES ROBINSON.

WHEREAS by the Proclamation annexed to Her Majesty's Order in Council dated the 18th day of June, 1869, it is ordained and declared that from and after a day to be fixed by the Governor or Officer Administering the Government of Ceylon, by Proclamation, and subject to further directions to be given by Proclamation of the Governor, the British and local copper or bronze coins or tokens at present in circulation in Her Majesty's Colony of Ceylon and its Dependencies, and such other copper or bronze tokens as may from time to time be specified by the Governor by Proclamation, shall be a legal tender of payment for any sum not exceeding half a Rupee; the said British and local coins to continue current until the date of such Proclamation, at the same rates, as regards the Rupee, as those at which they at present pass by long-established usage and custom, viz. :—

The Penny	at the rate of	$\frac{2}{3}$rds	of an Anna, or	8 Pie.
„ Half-penny	„	$\frac{1}{3}$rd	„	4 „
„ Farthing	„	$\frac{1}{6}$th	„	2 „
„ Ceylon Fanam	„	1	Anna.	
„ Stiver or Pice	„	$\frac{1}{4}$th	of an Anna, or	3 „
„ Challie	„	1/12th	„	1 „

And whereas it is expedient and desirable to establish certain other copper or bronze coins or tokens, representing certain decimal parts of a Rupee, as a legal tender for payment for any sum not exceeding half a Rupee.

And whereas there will shortly be issued by the Government of Ceylon, copper or bronze coins or tokens, as follows :—

A copper or bronze five-cent piece, representing one-twentieth part of a Rupee.

A copper or bronze one-cent piece, representing one-hundredth part of a Rupee.

A copper or bronze half-cent piece, representing one two-hundredth part of a Rupee.

And every such piece shall have for the obverse impression the effigy of Her Majesty, with the inscription " Victoria, Queen," and for the reverse impression the representation of a Talipot Palm and an inscription indicating the value of the piece in cents of a Rupee, with the word " Ceylon," and the date of the year, and words indicating the value in Sinhalese and Tamil :

Now, therefore, We, the said Governor, in pursuance and exercise of the authority vested in Us by the aforesaid Proclamation, do hereby proclaim and direct that the said copper or bronze coins or tokens so to be issued as aforesaid, shall from and after the First day of January, 1872, be lawfully current, and shall pass and be received as current and lawful tokens and payment within the Island of Ceylon and the Dependencies thereof, at and for the rates and values indicated thereon, and at no other rates or values. Provided, however, that no person shall be required to receive more than one half-Rupee in copper or bronze coins or tokens at one time.

And We do hereby further proclaim and direct, that until further lawful proclamation and direction to the contrary, the British and local copper or bronze coins or tokens now current in this Colony shall continue (subject to what is herein provided and directed) to pass and be received as current and lawful tokens and legal tender for payment, at the rates and values following, that is to say :—

The Penny at the rate of 1/24 of a Rupee.
,, Half-penny ,, 1/48th ,,
,, Farthing ,, 1/96th ,,
,, Ceylon Fanam ,, 1/16th ,,
,, Stiver or Pice ,, 1/64th ,,
,, Challie ,, 1/192nd ,,

Given at Colombo, in the said Island of Ceylon, this Twenty-third day of August, in the year of Our Lord One thousand Eight hundred and Seventy-one.

By His Excellency's command,

CHARLES P. LAYARD,
Acting Colonial Secretary.

GOD SAVE THE QUEEN.

(The *Ceylon Government Gazette* No. 3,836 of August 26, 1871.)

APPENDIX E.

In the Name of Her Majesty VICTORIA, of the United Kingdom of Great Britain and Ireland Queen, Defender of the Faith.

PROCLAMATION.

By His Excellency Sir Arthur Elibank Havelock, Knight Commander of the Most Distinguished Order of Saint Michael and Saint George, Governor and Commander-in-Chief in and over the Island of Ceylon, with the Dependencies thereof.

A. E. Havelock.

Whereas We have received from the Right Hon. the Secretary of State for the Colonies directions to proclaim Her Majesty's Order in Council, as follows :—

At the Court at Osborne House, Isle of Wight, the 6th day of February, 1892.

Present :

The Queen's Most Excellent Majesty.

Lord President. Mr. Ritchie. Mr. Jackson.

Whereas Her Majesty the Queen has power to make laws for the peace, order, and good government of Her Majesty's Colony of Ceylon ;

And whereas by virtue of the Order in Council and Proclamation rescinded by this Order certain silver rupees and other coins of silver and copper are legal tender in Her Majesty's said Colony ;

And whereas it appears to Her Majesty, by the advice of Her Privy Council, that it is expedient to rescind the said Proclamation, and to make a law respecting the coins which are to be the subject of contract, and to constitute legal tender in Her Majesty's said Colony ;

Now therefore Her Majesty, by and with the advice of Her Privy Council, and by virtue of all powers vested in Her Majesty in that behalf, doth hereby ordain that the law hereinafter mentioned shall take effect in Her Majesty's said Colony.

And the Lords Commissioners of Her Majesty's Treasury and the Right Honourable Lord Knutsford, one of Her Majesty's Principal Secretaries of State, are to give the requisite directions for causing proclamation of the said law to be made in Her Majesty's said Colony.

1. (1) The silver rupee of British India of the standard weight and millesimal fineness specified in the first schedule to this Order shall be the standard coin of Her Majesty's Colony of Ceylon and its dependencies, in this Order referred to as the Colony.

(2) Every contract, sale, payment, bill, note, instrument, and security for money, and every transaction, dealing, matter, and thing whatever relating to money, or involving the payment of, or the liability to, pay any money, shall, in the absence of express agreement to the contrary, be held to be made, executed, entered into, done, and had in the Colony according to the standard coin of the Colony.

(3) The coin mentioned in the second schedule to this Order shall be treated as equal to the standard coin.*

---

* See Order in Council dated July 17, 1893.

2. (1) Subsidiary coins may be from time to time coined for the Colony under the direction of the Master of Her Majesty's Mint or at one of Her Majesty's Mints in British India, of the denominations, weights, and fineness specified in the third schedule to this Order.

(2) Those coins shall have for the obverse impression Her Majesty's effigy with the inscription "Victoria Queen" and for the reverse impression the representation of a talipot palm and an inscription with the word "Ceylon," and the date of the year, and with the value of the piece in cents or hundredths of a rupee indicated in English, Sinhalese, and Tamil.

(3) Each coin so coined shall be a legal tender for the amount of its denomination.

(4) Each of the subsidiary coins mentioned in the fourth schedule to this Order shall be a legal tender for the amount in that behalf in that schedule mentioned.

3. (1) If the Governor of the Colony from time to time requests any new coins of less value than the rupee, whether of silver, copper, or mixed metal to be coined, and the Commissioners of Her Majesty's Treasury approve such request, those new coins may be so coined under the direction of the Master of Her Majesty's Mint, or at one of Her Majesty's Mints in British India.

(2) Such new coins shall have either the impressions* directed by this Order for the coins specified in the third schedule (in this Order referred to as existing coins), or such other impressions as may be approved of by the Master of Her Majesty's Mint and the Commissioners of Her Majesty's Treasury.

(3) Any such new coin may be of the same denomination as any existing coin, or of a different denomination.

(4) Every such new coin, if of silver, shall be of the same fineness as the existing silver coins, and of a weight bearing the same proportion to the weights of the existing silver coins as the denomination of the new coin bears to the denominations of the existing coins.

4. In the making of any existing or new coin a "remedy" or variation from the standard weight, and in the case of silver coins from the standard fineness required by this Order, shall be allowed for any existing coin of an amount not exceeding that specified in the third schedule to this Order, and for any new coin—

(*a*) As regards fineness (if the coin is of silver) of the amount specified in the third schedule to this Order; and

(*b*) As regards weight of an amount bearing the same proportion: (1) if of silver to the weight of the twenty-five cent piece mentioned in the said schedule; and (2) if of copper or mixed metal to the weight of the five-cent piece mentioned in the said schedule, as the denomination of the new coin bears to those pieces respectively.

5. (1) A tender of payment of money in the Colony if made in standard coins or in any coins specified in the second, third, or fourth schedule to this Order, shall—provided that the coins have not been illegally dealt with, and provided that, in the case of silver coins, such coins have not become diminished in weight by wear or otherwise so as to be of less weight than the weight (if any) specified as the least current weight in the schedules to this Order—be a legal tender

(*a*) In the case of rupees, for the payment of any amount;

* The substitution of the effigy of one Sovereign for that of another does not make the coins "new" coins for the purpose of this Order—Chalmers.

(*b*) In the case of other silver coins, for the payment of an amount not exceeding five rupees, but for no greater amount ;

(*c*) In the case of coins of copper or mixed metal, for the payment of an amount not exceeding one-half of a rupee, but for no greater amount.

(2) If any new coins are coined, this article shall, after the date fixed by the Governor—in a Proclamation made with the approval of the Commissioners of Her Majesty's Treasury and one of Her Majesty's Principal Secretaries of State, and setting forth in a schedule the same particulars with respect to each coin as are set forth in the third schedule to this Order, apply to the new coins as if the schedule to the Proclamation were added to that third schedule.

6. For the purpose of this Order a coin shall be deemed to have been illegally dealt with where the coin has been impaired, diminished, or lightened otherwise than by fair wear and tear, or has been defaced by having any name, word, device, or number stamped thereon, whether the coin has or has not been thereby diminished or lightened.

7. On the commencement of this Order, the Order in Council and Proclamation specified in the fifth schedule to this Order, and all such Colonial laws and all such Proclamations, whether issued by Her Majesty or by the Governor, as regulate legal tender in the Colony, other than "The Ceylon Paper Currency Ordinance, 1884" (No. 32 of 1884), shall cease to be in force.

8. Nothing in this Order, nor any repeal of laws or rescinding of Proclamations by this Order, shall affect any liability incurred, contract made, or other thing done before the commencement of this Order.

9. In this Order—

The expression "Governor" means the Governor of the Colony, and includes the Officer for the time being administering the Government of the Colony.

Words in the singular include the plural, and words in the plural include the singular.

10. This Order shall come into operation on the First day of July, 1892*, or any earlier day on which it is proclaimed in the Colony by the Governor, and that day is in this Order referred to as the commencement of the Order.

11. This Order may be cited as the Coinage (Ceylon) Order, 1892.

C. L. PEEL.

FIRST SCHEDULE.

Standard Coin.

Coin.	Metal.	Millesimal Fineness.	Standard Weight.		Least Current Weight.	
			Grains	Grammes	Grains	Grammes
Rupee of British India ..	Silver	916·6	180	11·664	176·4	11·431

* Altered to October 1, 1892, by Amending Order in Council dated June 28, 1892.

SECOND SCHEDULE.

Foreign Coin.*

Ratio to Standard Coin.	Coin.	Metal.	Millesimal Fineness.	Standard Weight.		Least Current Weight.	
				Grains	Grammes	Grains	Grammes
1·0	Rupee of Portuguese India	Silver	916·6̇	180	11·664	176·4	11·431

* Demonetized by Order in Council of July 17, 1893.

THIRD SCHEDULE.

Subsidiary Coins of Ceylon.

Portion of Rupee for which Tender.	Coin.	Metal.	Millesimal Fineness.	Standard Weight.		Remedy Allowances.		
						Weight per piece.		Millesimal Fineness.
				Grains	Grammes.	Grains.	Grammes.	
0·5	Ceylon Fifty-cent piece ..	Silver	800	90	5·832	0·630	0·0408	3
0·25	Ceylon Twenty-five cent piece ..	,,	800	45	2·916	0·315	0·0204	3
0·10	Ceylon Ten-cent piece	,,	800	18	1·166	0·18	0·0117	3
0·05*	Ceylon Five-cent piece	Copper or mixed metal	—	291·6̇	18·9	7·29	0·472	None
0·01	Ceylon One-cent piece		—	72·916	4·725	1·82	0·118	,,
0·005	Ceylon Half-cent piece		—	36·458	2·362	0·91	0·059	,,
0·0025†	Ceylon Quarter-cent piece		—	18·229	1·181	0·46	0·029	,,

* Amended by Proclamation of December 13, 1909—nickel coin substituted.
† Demonetized by Order in Council of October 18, 1909.

FOURTH SCHEDULE.

Subsidiary Coins not of Ceylon.

Portion of Rupee for which Tender	Coin.	Metal.	Millesimal Fineness.	Standard Weight.		Least Current Weight.	
				Grains.	Grammes	Grains	Grammes
0·5	Half rupee or Eight-anna piece of British India	Silver	916·6̇	90	5·832	88·2	5·715
0·25	Quarter rupee or Four-anna piece of British India ..	,,	916·6̇	45	2·916	44·1	2·858

FIFTH SCHEDULE.

Order in Council and Proclamation rescinded.

June 18, 1869 : Order in Council and Proclamation.

Now therefore We, the said Governor of Ceylon, in pursuance and exercise of the authority vested in Us by the said Order in Council, do hereby proclaim and direct that the said Order in Council shall and do take effect and come into force in Her Majesty's Colony of Ceylon, and the Dependencies thereof, from and after the First day of July, 1892.

Given at Kandy, in the said Island of Ceylon, this Twenty-third day of June, in the year of Our Lord One thousand Eight hundred and Ninety-two.

By His Excellency's command,

J. A. SWETTENHAM,
Acting Colonial Secretary.

GOD SAVE THE QUEEN.

(The *Ceylon Government Gazette Extraordinary* of June 25, 1892.)

APPENDIX F.

HIS Excellency the Lieutenant-Governor has been pleased to direct that the subjoined copy of the Order of Her Majesty in Council dated July 17, 1893, amending the Coinage (Ceylon) Order, 1892, by demonetizing the rupee of Portuguese India in Ceylon, be published for general information.

By His Excellency's command,

Colonial Secretary's Office,
Colombo, August 17, 1893.

J. A. SWETTENHAM,
Acting Colonial Secretary.

At the Court at Windsor, the 17th day of July, 1893.

Present:

THE QUEEN'S MOST EXCELLENT MAJESTY.

Lord President.
Lord Steward.
Marquess of Ripon.
Sir Edmund Monson.

WHEREAS by the Coinage (Ceylon) Order, 1892, Her Majesty was pleased by and with the advice of Her Privy Council, to make a law respecting the coin constituting legal tender in Her Majesty's Colony of Ceylon :

And whereas by such Order it was, *inter alia*, declared that a tender of payment of money in the said Colony if made in the rupee of Portuguese India, being the coin specified in the second schedule to such Order, should be a legal tender in the said Colony :

And whereas it is deemed expedient that the last-mentioned provision of such Order should be repealed :

Now therefore Her Majesty, by and with the advice of Her Privy Council, and by virtue of all powers vested in Her Majesty in that behalf, doth hereby ordain and declare as follows :—

1. A tender of payment of money in the Colony of Ceylon, if made in the rupee of Portuguese India, shall, from and after the 19th day of July,

1893, cease to be a legal tender, and so much of the Coinage (Ceylon) Order, 1892, as makes tender of payment in such coin a legal tender shall, as from the said 19th day of July, 1893, be, and is hereby repealed.

2. At any time within such period after the 19th day of July, 1893, as the Governor of the Colony shall by Proclamation appoint, rupees of Portuguese India will be received at any Government Treasury in the Colony, and will be exchanged for rupees of British India.

The Lords Commissioners of Her Majesty's Treasury and the Marquess of Ripon, one of Her Majesty's Principal Secretaries of State, are to give the requisite directions for causing this Order to be proclaimed in the Colony.

C. L. PEEL.

(The *Ceylon Government Gazette Extraordinary* of July 19, 1893.)

APPENDIX G.

IN the name of His Majesty EDWARD THE SEVENTH of the United Kingdom of Great Britain and Ireland King, Defender of the Faith

PROCLAMATION.

By His Excellency the Right Honourable SIR J. WEST RIDGEWAY, Knight Grand Cross of the Most Distinguished Order of Saint Michael and Saint George, Knight Commander of the Most Honourable Order of the Bath, Knight Commander of the Most Exalted Order of the Star of India, Governor and Commander-in-Chief in and over the Island of Ceylon, with the Dependencies thereof.

WEST RIDGEWAY.

WHEREAS We have received from the Right Honourable the Secretary of State for the Colonies directions to proclaim His Majesty's Order in Council, as follows :—

At the Court at St. James' the 26th day of September, 1901.

THE KING'S MOST EXCELLENT MAJESTY.

Lord George Hamilton.	Mr. St. John Brodrick.
Mr. Chamberlain.	Sir Charles Scott.

WHEREAS by an Order in Council dated the 6th day of February, 1892, Her late Majesty Queen Victoria was pleased, by and with the advice of Her Privy Council, to make a law respecting the coin constituting legal tender in the Colony of Ceylon :

And whereas it is expedient to amend the aforesaid Order by constituting the sovereign a legal tender in the said Colony :

Now therefore, His Majesty the King, by and with the advice of His Privy Council, and by virtue of all powers vested in His Majesty in that behalf, doth hereby ordain and declare as follows :—

1. A tender of payment of money, if made in sovereigns which have been issued by His Majesty's Royal Mint in England or by any branch of that Mint for the time being established, and have not been called in by any

Proclamation made in pursuance of The Coinage Act, 1870, and have not been diminished in weight by wear or otherwise so as to be of less weight than the weight specified or declared for the purpose by or in pursuance of the said Act, shall be legal tender in His Majesty's Colony of Ceylon for a payment of any amount at the rate of one sovereign for fifteen rupees.

2. This Order may be cited as The Coinage (Ceylon) Amendment Order in Council, 1901, and shall come into force upon the date to be fixed in that behalf by Proclamation of the Governor in Council.

The Lords Commissioners of His Majesty's Treasury and the Right Honourable Joseph Chamberlain, one of His Majesty's Principal Secretaries of State, are to give the requisite directions for causing this Order to be proclaimed in His Majesty's said Colony.

A. W. FITZROY.

Now therefore, We, the said Governor of Ceylon in Council, in pursuance and exercise of the authority vesting in Us by the said Order in Council, do hereby proclaim and direct that the said Order in Council shall and do take effect and come into force in His Majesty's Colony of Ceylon and the Dependencies thereof from and after the 25th day of October, 1901.

Given at Colombo, in the said Island of Ceylon, this Twenty-fifth day of October, in the year of our Lord One thousand Nine hundred and One.

By His Excellency's command,

W. T. TAYLOR,
Acting Colonial Secretary.

GOD SAVE THE KING.

APPENDIX H.

At the Court at Buckingham Palace, the 18th day of October, 1909.

Present :

THE KING'S MOST EXCELLENT MAJESTY,

Lord President. Mr. Samuel.
Master of the Horse. Sir Hudson Kearley.
Lord Sandhurst. Mr. James Stuart.

WHEREAS His Majesty has power to make laws for the peace, order, and good government of the Colony of Ceylon (in this Order referred to as the Colony) :

And whereas by virtue of the Coinage (Ceylon) Order, 1892, the Ceylon five-cent piece and the Ceylon quarter-cent piece, being two of the subsidiary coins specified in the Third Schedule to the said Order, are legal tender in the Colony :

And whereas it is expedient that the said five cent piece and the said quarter-cent piece should no longer be legal tender in the Colony :

NOW THEREFORE, His Majesty by virtue of all powers vested in Him in that behalf, is pleased, by and with the advice of His Privy Council, to order, and it is hereby ordered, as follows :—

1. The Ceylon five-cent piece and the Ceylon quarter-cent piece specified in the Third Schedule to the Coinage (Ceylon) Order, 1892, shall cease to be current or legal tender in the Colony.

2. This Order shall be read as one with the Coinage (Ceylon) Order, 1892, and the Orders amending that Order, and may be cited as the Ceylon (Coinage) Order, 1909.

(2) This Order shall come into operation upon the date to be fixed in that behalf by proclamation of the Governor of the Colony in Council.

And the Lords Commissioners of His Majesty's Treasury and the Right Honourable the Earl of Crewe, K.G., one of His Majesty's Principal Secretaries of State, are to give the requisite directions therein accordingly.

ALMERIC FITZROY.

IN the Name of His Majesty EDWARD THE SEVENTH, of the United Kingdom of Great Britain and Ireland and of the British Dominions beyond the Seas, King, Defender of the Faith.

PROCLAMATION.

By His Excellency SIR HENRY EDWARD MCCALLUM, Knight Grand Cross of the Most Distinguished Order of Saint Michael and Saint George, Governor and Commander-in-Chief in and over the Island of Ceylon, with the Dependencies thereof.

HENRY MCCALLUM.

WHEREAS by virtue of the Coinage (Ceylon) Order, 1892, the Ceylon five-cent piece and the Ceylon quarter-cent piece, being two of the subsidiary coins specified in the third schedule to the said Order, are legal tender in Ceylon:

And whereas by the Ceylon (Coinage) Order, 1909, His Majesty, by and with the advice of His Privy Council, has been pleased to order—

(1) That the Ceylon five-cent piece and the Ceylon quarter-cent piece specified in the third schedule to the Coinage (Ceylon) Order, 1892, shall cease to be current or legal tender in the Colony;

(2) That the said Order should come into operation upon the date to be fixed in that behalf by Proclamation of the Governor of the Colony in Council:

Now therefore, We, the said Governor of Ceylon, in pursuance of the said Ceylon (Coinage) Order, 1909, and with the advice of the Executive Council, do by this Our Proclamation direct that the said Ceylon (Coinage) Order, 1909, shall come into operation upon the First day of July, 1910.

Given at Colombo, in the said Island of Ceylon, this Thirteenth day of December, in the year of Our Lord One thousand Nine hundred and Nine.

By His Excellency's command,

HUGH CLIFFORD,
Colonial Secretary.

GOD SAVE THE KING.

(The *Ceylon Government Gazette* No. 6,346 of December 17, 1909.)

APPENDIX I.

In the Name of His Majesty EDWARD THE SEVENTH, of the United Kingdom of Great Britain and Ireland and of the British Dominions beyond the Seas, King, Defender of the Faith.

PROCLAMATION.

By His Excellency Sir Henry Edward McCallum, Knight Grand Cross of the Most Distinguished Order of Saint Michael and Saint George, Governor and Commander-in-Chief in and over the Island of Ceylon, with the Dependencies thereof.

Henry McCallum.

Whereas by an Order of Her late Majesty in Council dated February 6, 1892, it was amongst other things provided that subsidiary coins might be from time to time coined for Ceylon under the direction of the Master of Her Majesty's Mint or at one of Her Majesty's Mints, in British India of the denominations, weights, and fineness specified in the third schedule to the said Order, and that those coins should have the obverse and reverse impressions specified in Article 2 of the said Order, and that each such coin should be a legal tender for the amount of its denomination :

And whereas by the said Order it was further provided that if the Governor of Ceylon from time to time requests any new coins of less value than the rupee, whether of silver, copper, or mixed metal, to be coined, and the Commissioners of Her Majesty's Treasury approve such request, those new coins might be so coined under the direction of the Master of Her Majesty's Mint or at one of Her Majesty's Mints in British India, and that such new coins should have either the impressions directed by the said Order for the coins specified in the third schedule thereof or such other impressions as might be approved by the Master of Her Majesty's Mint and the Commissioners of Her Majesty's Treasury :

And whereas We, the aforesaid Governor of Ceylon, have requested that a new subsidiary coin should be coined of the denomination, value, composition, weight, and fineness set out in the schedule hereto, and the Commissioners of His Majesty's Treasury have approved of such request, and the said new subsidiary coin has been coined having for the obverse impression His Majesty's effigy with the inscription "Edward the Seventh, King and Emperor," and for the reverse impression that specified in the second clause of Article 2 of the said Order, which impressions have been approved of by the Master of His Majesty's Mint and the Commissioners of His Majesty's Treasury :

And whereas by Article 5 of the said Order it was provided amongst other things that, subject to the conditions in the said article contained a tender of payment of money in Ceylon should, in the case of coins of copper and mixed metal, be legal tender for the payment of an amount not exceeding one-half of a rupee, but for no greater amount ; and by the said article it was further provided that if any new coins were coined, the said article should, after the date fixed by the Governor in a Proclamation made with the approval of the Commissioners of Her Majesty's Treasury and one of Her Majesty's principal Secretaries of State, and setting forth the same particulars with respect to such coin as were set forth in the third schedule to the said Order, apply to the new coins as if the schedule to the Proclamation were added to the third schedule :

Now know Ye that We, the aforesaid Governor of Ceylon, hereby in pursuance of Article 5 of the above recited Order of Her late Majesty in Council, and with the approval of the Commissioners of His Majesty's

Treasury and one of His Majesty's principal Secretaries of State, proclaim and direct that from and after January 1, 1910, Article 5 of the above recited Order of Her late Majesty in Council, dated February 6, 1892, shall apply to the subsidiary coin, the particulars whereof are set forth in the schedule hereto.

Given at Colombo, in the said Island of Ceylon, this Thirteenth day of December, in the year of Our Lord One thousand Nine hundred and Nine.

By His Excellency's command,

HUGH CLIFFORD,
Colonial Secretary.

GOD SAVE THE KING.

SCHEDULE.

Portion of Rupee for which Tender.	Coin.	Metal.	Millesimal Fineness.	Standard Weight.		Remedy Allowance.	
				Grains.	Grammes.	Weight.	Millesimal Fineness.
0·05	Ceylon Five-cent piece ..	Nickel bronze	—	60	3·888	A weight not exceeding the weight of one piece in every forty pieces ..	None

(The *Ceylon Government Gazette* No. 6,346 of December 17, 1909.)

APPENDIX J.

IN the Name of His Majesty GEORGE THE FIFTH, of the United Kingdom of Great Britain and Ireland and of the British Dominions beyond the Seas, King, Defender of the Faith.

PROCLAMATION.

By His Excellency SIR WILLIAM HENRY MANNING, Knight Commander of the Most Distinguished Order of Saint Michael and Saint George, Knight Commander of the Most Excellent Order of the British Empire, Companion of the Most Honourable Order of the Bath, Governor and Commander-in-Chief in and over the Island of Ceylon, with the Dependencies thereof.

W. H. MANNING.

WHEREAS We have received from the Right Honourable the Secretary of State for the Colonies directions to proclaim His Majesty's Order in Council, as follows :—

At the Court at Buckingham Palace, the 8th day of May, 1919.

Present:

THE KING'S MOST EXCELLENT MAJESTY.

Chancellor of the Duchy of Lancaster
Lord Steward.
Lord Colebrooke.
Lord Southborough.

Whereas His Majesty the King has power to make laws for the peace, order, and good government of His Majesty's Colony of Ceylon:

And whereas by the Coinage (Ceylon) Order, 1892, a law was made respecting the coins which were to be the subject of contract and to constitute legal tender in His Majesty's said Colony:

And whereas it is expedient to amend the said Order with respect to the millesimal fineness and remedy allowance in respect of certain of the subsidiary coins specified in the Third Schedule to the said Order:

Now, therefore, His Majesty, by and with the advice of His Privy Council, and by virtue of all powers vested in His Majesty in that behalf, doth hereby ordain and declare as follows:—

1. (1) 550 shall be substituted for 800 in the fourth column of the Third Schedule to the Coinage (Ceylon) Order, 1892, as the millesimal fineness of Ceylon fifty-cent, twenty-five cent, and ten-cent pieces coined after such date as may be fixed by the Governon of the Colony by Proclamation.

(2) 5 shall be substituted for 3 in the last column of the said Third Schedule as the corresponding remedy allowance for those coins.

2. The Governor of the Colony may, by Proclamation made with the approval of the Commissioners of His Majesty's Treasury and one of His Majesty's Principal Secretaries of State, declare that Ceylon fifty-cent, twenty-five cent, and ten-cent pieces coined up to and including such date as may have been fixed by Proclamation under sub-section (1) of section 1 of this Order shall cease to be legal tender, notwithstanding anything in the Coinage (Ceylon) Order, 1892, and the Orders amending that Order.

3. The Interpretation Act, 1889, shall apply for the purpose of the Interpretation of this Order, as it applies for the purpose of the interpretation of an Act of Parliament.

4. This Order may be cited as the Coinage (Ceylon) Order, 1919, and shall be construed as one with the Coinage (Ceylon) Order, 1892, and the Orders amending that Order: and the Coinage (Ceylon) Order, 1892, the Orders in Council of the 28th day of June, 1892, and the 17th day of July, 1893, amending that Order, the Coinage (Ceylon) Amendment Order in Council, 1901, the Ceylon (Coinage) Order, 1909, and this Order may be cited together as the Coinage (Ceylon) Orders, 1892 to 1919.

And the Lords Commissioners of His Majesty's Treasury and the Right Honourable Viscount Milner, one of His Majesty's Principal Secretaries of State, are to give the requisite directions for causing this Order to be proclaimed in His Majesty's said Colony.

ALMERIC FITZROY.

Now therefore, We, the said Governor of Ceylon, do hereby proclaim the said Order in Council, and do further by this Proclamation fix the First day of September, 1919, as the date which may be fixed by Us in pursuance of the power vested in Us under sub-section (1) of section 1 of the said Order in Council.

Given at Colombo, in the said Island of Ceylon, this Twenty-ninth day of August, in the year of our Lord One thousand Nine hundred and Nineteen.

By His Excellency's command,

A. S. PAGDEN,
Acting Colonial Secretary.

(The *Ceylon Government Gazette* No. 7,048 of August 29, 1919.)

APPENDIX K.

At the Court at Buckingham Palace, the 13th day of August, 1920.

Present:

THE KING'S MOST EXCELLENT MAJESTY IN COUNCIL.

WHEREAS His Majesty has power to make laws for the peace, order and good government of the Colony of Ceylon (in this Order referred to as "the Colony"):

And whereas by virtue of the Coinage (Ceylon) Amendment Order in Council, 1901 (in this Order referred to as "the Order of 1901"), the sovereign is legal tender in the Colony:

And whereas it is expedient that the sovereign should no longer be legal tender in the Colony:

Now, therefore, His Majesty, by virtue of all powers vested in him in that behalf, is pleased, by and with the advice of His Privy Council to order, and it is hereby ordered, as follows:—

1. The sovereign shall cease to be current or legal tender in the Colony.

2. (1) This Order may be cited as the Ceylon (Coinage) Order, 1920.

(2) This Order shall be deemed to have had effect as from the 7th day of August, 1920.

And the Lords Commissioners of His Majesty's Treasury, and the Right Honourable Viscount Milner, G.C.B., G.C.M.G., one of His Majesty's Principal Secretaries of State, are to give the requisite directions herein accordingly.

ALMERIC FITZROY.

IN the Name of His Majesty GEORGE THE FIFTH, of the United Kingdom of Great Britain and Ireland and of the British Dominions beyond the Seas, King, Defender of the Faith.

PROCLAMATION.

By His Excellency Sir GRAEME THOMSON, Knight Commander of the Most Honourable Order of the Bath, Officer Administering the Government of the Island of Ceylon, with the Dependencies thereof.

GRAEME THOMSON.

WHEREAS His Majesty, by and with the advice of his Privy Council, has been pleased to direct that a sovereign shall cease to be currency or legal tender in the Colony as and from the date of this Proclamation.

Now, therefore, know Ye that We, the Officer Administering the Government, do hereby proclaim and direct that the said Order in Council shall and do take effect and come into force in this Colony of Ceylon and the Dependencies thereof as and from the date hereof.

Given at Colombo, in the said Island of Ceylon, this Seventh day of August, in the year of our Lord One thousand Nine hundred and Twenty.

By His Excellency's Command,

B. HORSBURGH,
Acting Colonial Secretary.

GOD SAVE THE KING.

(The *Ceylon Government Gazette Extraordinary* No. 7,121, Saturday, August 7, 1920.)

APPENDIX L.

PAPER CURRENCY.

Ordinances Nos. 32 of 1884, 12 of 1886, 13 of 1901, 6 of 1903, 11 of 1909, 33 of 1914, 1 of 1917.

AN ORDINANCE TO PROVIDE FOR THE ISSUE OF GOVERNMENT PAPER CURRENCY.

[*17th December*, 1884.]

Short title.

1. This Ordinance may be cited as the Paper Currency Ordinance, and it shall extend to the whole of the Island of Ceylon.

Commissioners of Currency.

2. A board of Commissioners of Currency for the Island shall be established for the purposes of this Ordinance, and shall consist of the Financial Secretary, the Deputy Chief Secretary, and the Commissioner of Stamps.

Board of Commissioners created a corporation under the style of "The Ceylon Currency Commissioners."

3. (1) The Board of Commissioners of Currency established under section 2 shall, from and after the first day of November eighteen hundred and eighty-six, be and become a corporation with continuance for ever, under the name and style of "The Ceylon Currency Commissioners," with full power and authority to have and to use a common seal, and change and alter the same at their will and pleasure, and shall and may perform each and every of the duties and exercise each and every of the powers imposed on and vested in them by this Ordinance; and all acts, matters or things which are authorised by this Ordinance to be done by them or in their names shall and may be lawfully done by them or in their name and style as a corporation:

Provided, however, that the seal of the said corporation shall not be fixed to any instrument except in the presence of at least one of the Commissioners, who shall sign his name to the instrument in token of his presence, and such signing shall be independent of the signing of any person who may sign the instrument as a witness.

Corporation may appoint officers or agents.

(2) The said corporation, with the sanction of the Governor, may from time to time under their common seal appoint such officer or officers, agent or agents, as they may consider necessary for recovering all dividends, interest, or other revenue to be derived from all lawful investments already made, or which may hereafter be made by them, or for otherwise carrying out the provisions of this Ordinance; and all persons so appointed shall hold office during the pleasure of the said corporation.

Commissioners may issue Government notes.

4. There shall be transferred to the Commissioners coin legally current, or coin and securities as hereafter provided, and thereupon it shall be lawful for the Commissioners from time to time to provide, issue, and re-issue promissory notes of the Government of Ceylon payable to bearer on demand equal to the whole amount of coin and securities in the hands of the Commissioners. Such notes shall be for the respective sums following, namely :—

One rupee,	Fifty rupees,
Two rupees,	One hundred rupees,
Five rupees,	Five hundred rupees,
Ten rupees,	One thousand rupees.

5. Every such note shall bear the signatures or facsimiles of the signatures of any two of the Commissioners holding office at the date borne on the note.

Notes to be signed by two Commissioners.

6. Such notes shall be called "currency notes," and shall be payable only at the office of the Commissioners in Colombo. The holders of currency notes shall be entitled to obtain on demand at the said office in exchange for such notes coin which may at the option of the Commissioners be either silver rupees of India or gold coin which is legal tender in Ceylon under any Order of His Majesty the King in Council, but no other coin.

Notes to be called "currency notes," and holders may demand coin for them.

7. Every currency note shall be legal tender in Ceylon for the payment of any amount.

Currency notes to be legal tender for any amount.

8. (1) The Commissioners shall, on the demand of any person, issue currency notes in exchange for the amount thereof in silver rupees of India.

Issue of currency notes.

(2) The Commissioners may also issue such notes in exchange for the amount thereof in gold coin which is legal tender in Ceylon under any Order of His Majesty the King in Council; but the Commissioners may decline to do so whenever it is inexpedient in their judgment to increase the amount of gold coin held as reserve under this Ordinance:

Provided that until such date as shall be notified by order of the Governor in the *Government Gazette*, it shall be lawful, and shall be deemed to have been lawful, for the Commissioners, with the approval of the Secretary of State, to treat an acceptance of a credit at the Bank of England to an amount so approved as equivalent to a deposit of such gold coin as aforesaid in accordance with this subsection, and in any such case the amount of such credit shall be deemed to be such gold coin as aforesaid for all the purposes of this Ordinance, except for the purposes of section 6.

Power to treat credit at Bank of England as equivalent to a deposit of gold.

9. The Commissioners shall retain a reserve in silver coin or in gold coin which is legal tender in this Island under any Order of His Majesty the King in Council, of one-half at the least of the amount of currency notes in circulation. The said reserve shall be from time to time, at such times as the Governor shall appoint, verified by a board of survey.

Commissioners to retain a reserve of one-half in silver or gold coin of the notes in circulation.

Governor to direct investment of one-half of the value of notes in circulation.

10. The Governor, shall also cause a sum, not exceeding the value of one-half of the currency notes in circulation, to be invested in Indian Government securities and such securities of the Government of the United Kingdom of Great Britain and Northern Ireland or of the Government of any British colony other than Ceylon, as may from time to time be approved of by the Secretary of State for the Colonies :

Provided that not more than one-half of such sum shall be invested in Indian Government securities, except by the express sanction of the Secretary of State.

Reserve to be set apart to satisfy notes.

11. The said reserve in coin and securities shall be appropriated and set apart to provide for the satisfaction and discharge of the said currency notes ; and the said currency notes shall be held to have been issued on the security of the said coin and securities as well as on the general credit of the Government of Ceylon.

How investments to be made.

12. All such investments shall, if made in England, be made in the joint names of the Crown Agents for the Colonies and of such other officers or persons as His Majesty's Secretary of State aforesaid shall appoint as trustees on behalf of the Commissioners. Investments made in India in Indian Government securities shall be made in the names of the Commissioners.

Investments may be sold or varied if directed by the Governor.

13. Any portion of the aforesaid investments may, if directed by the Governor, be sold by the persons in whose names they have been made, and the proceeds of such sale applied to keep up the aforesaid reserve of coin, or in the purchase of other securities authorised by this Ordinance.

When Commissioners will be authorised to sell out securities.

14. If at any time the specie held by the Commissioners as mentioned in section 9 should be reduced below one-half of the notes in circulation, it shall not be necessary for the Commissioners (except by the special directions of the Governor) to sell and realize any of the said securities, unless and until the amount of specie in their hands shall be less than one-third of the notes in circulation at the time :

Provided that no further investment in the said securities shall be made until the reserve mentioned in section 9 shall amount to one-half at the least of the amount of currency notes in circulation ;

Suspension of operation of proviso to this section.

Provided further that the operation of the above proviso shall be suspended, and shall be deemed to have been suspended, as from the thirtieth day of December, nineteen hundred and sixteen, until such date as shall be notified by order of the Governor in the *Government Gazette* ;

Provided further that during the said suspension the limit of the proportion of the value of currency notes in circulation which may be invested in securities under section 10 shall also be suspended, and be deemed to have been suspended, as from the said date.

15. All dividends, interest, or other revenue to be derived from the said investments shall be paid to such person as shall be nominated in that behalf, and the said dividends, interest, or revenue shall form part of the ordinary revenues of the Island, excepting the sum of one per centum which shall be appropriated annually on the whole amount of such investments, and shall be paid to the trustees referred to in section 12, to be by them invested in such manner as the Governor, with the sanction of the Secretary of State, shall approve : **Revenue from investments.**

Provided always that the Governor may, with the sanction of the said Secretary of State, direct that the annual appropriations of one per centum aforesaid shall be wholly or partially discontinued at any time, or so long as it shall appear that the reason for such annual appropriation no longer exists. Investments made in pursuance of this section shall be deemed to form part of the reserve mentioned in section 11, and shall be held and dealt with in the manner prescribed by sections 12, 13, and 14 of this Ordinance.

16. An account showing the amount of the profits of the note circulation and of the charges and expenses incidental thereto shall be made and published annually in the *Government Gazette*. **Accounts showing expenses to be published annually in *Government Gazette*.**

17. An abstract of the accounts of the Commissioners showing— **Accounts showing amount of notes in circulation, &c., to be published monthly in the *Government Gazette*.**

(*a*) the whole amount of currency notes in circulation ;
(*b*) the amount of silver and gold coin reserved ; and
(*c*) the nominal value as well as the latest known market price of, and the price paid for, the Government securities held by the Commissioners,

shall be made up on the tenth day of each month by the Commissioners, and published as soon as may be in the *Government Gazette*.

18. Whosoever shall forge or counterfeit or alter, or shall offer, utter, dispose of, or put off, knowing the same to be forged or counterfeited or altered, any currency note or any word, figure, mark, sign, signature, or facsimile upon or attached to any such note, shall be held guilty of an offence, and shall on conviction be liable to imprisonment, with or without hard labour, for any period not exceeding twenty years, anything in the Penal Code to the contrary notwithstanding. **Penalty for counterfeiting notes.**

19. Whosoever without lawful authority or excuse (the proof whereof shall lie on the person accused) shall have in his possession any such forged, counterfeited, or altered note, or any unfinished or incomplete note purporting to be issued by the Commissioners, shall be guilty of an offence, and be liable to imprisonment, with or without hard labour, for any period not exceeding five years, anything in the Penal Code to the contrary notwithstanding. **Penalty for possession of incomplete notes.**

Penalty for possession of paper for notes.

20. Whosoever without lawful authority or excuse (the proof whereof shall lie on the person accused) shall make, use, or knowingly have in his possession, any paper with any word, figure, device, or distinction peculiar to and appearing in the substance of the paper used for currency notes, or any frame, mould, or instrument for making such paper, or any material upon which the whole or any part of any note purporting to resemble a currency note shall have been engraved or made, or any facsimile of the signature of any of the Commissioners, shall be guilty of an offence, and shall be liable on conviction to imprisonment, with or without hard labour, for any period not exceeding five years, anything in the Penal Code to the contrary notwithstanding.

Certificate under the hand of the Deputy Financial Secretary to be conclusive evidence as to the spuriousness of certain currency notes.

21. (1) In any proceedings in which the genuineness of any currency note shall be in question, a certificate under the hand of the Deputy Financial Secretary to the effect that such note is spurious, on the ground that it does not contain the secret features characteristic of a genuine note of corresponding denomination, number, and date shall be received in all courts of law as conclusive evidence of the spuriousness of such note.

(2) The Deputy Financial Secretary shall not be examined or cross-examined with respect to any such certificate.

(3) The certificate shall be in the form following :

> This to certify that I have personally examined the document shown to me, and marked ———, purporting to be a currency note of the following denomination, number, and date, namely—
>
> Denomination : ———
> Number : ———
> Date : ———
>
> and that the said note is spurious on the ground that it does not contain the secret features characteristic of a genuine note of corresponding denomination, number, and date.

Interpretation.

22. The expressions "Financial Secretary," "Deputy Chief Secretary," "Deputy Financial Secretary" and "Commissioner of Stamps" means the persons for the time being lawfully discharging the functions of such officers, and the expression "the Commissioners" means the Commissioners of Currency by this Ordinance.

(Chapter 291, Legislative Enactments of Ceylon, 1938.)

APPENDIX M.

Note Circulation, Reserve, Currency Profits, &c. (000 omitted except in column 6).

Date.		Notes in Circulation.	Reserve.			Currency Profits.
			Metallic.	Securities.		
				Cost.	Market Value.	
		Rs.	Rs.	Rs.	Rs.	Rs.
31.12.1886	..	5,012	—	—	—	—
31.12.1887	..	5,171	2,930	2,267	—	—
31.12.1888	..	5,530	2,864	2,666	—	—
1.10.1890	..	5,564	2,505	3.059	—	—
1.10.1895	..	9,180	4,869	4,311	—	—
1.10.1898	..	11,278	5,665	5,613	—	—
1.10.1904	..	13,708	7,080	6,628	—	—
1.10.1908	..	15,007	6,371	8,636	—	—
1.10.1910	..	22,733	12,665	10,068	—	—
1.10.1911	..	22,642	11,779	10,863	—	—
1.10.1912	..	22,791	11,293	11,498	—	—
1.10.1913	..	28,945	14,884	14,061	—	—
1.10.1914	..	27,902	12,741	15,161	—	—
1.10.1915	..	27,325	12,164	15,161	—	—
1.10.1916	..	27,885	12,724	15,161	—	—
1.10.1917	..	38,875	19,564	19,311	—	—
1.10.1918	..	37,340	18,029	19,311	—	—
1.10.1919	..	40,533	19,222	21,311	—	—
1.10.1920	..	47,190	16,311	33,432	—	—
1.10.1921	..	45,734	14,855	28,264	—	—
1.10.1922	..	39,286	14,863	25,145	—	—
1.10.1923	..	39,705	15,272	26,238	28,560	1,059,979
1.10.1924	..	47,002	22,569	30,336	27,914	1,277,433
1.10.1925	..	52,976	26,549	32,340	30,087	1,378,091
1.10.1926	..	61,726	26,299	42,604	40,929	2,480,754
1.10.1927	..	62,475	25,047	44,836	42,533	2,013,471
1.10.1928	..	57,436	22,509	42,477	40,119	2,058,483
1.10.1929	..	57,328	22,401	39,770	38,907	1,945,349
1.10.1930	..	57,219	22,292	39,656	39,199	1,467,219
1.10.1931	..	42,441	14,264	33,057	32,187	1,713,154
1.10.1932	..	41,967	13,790	33,216	35,340	1,487,713
1.10.1933	..	42,029	13,852	33,731	37,403	1,988,970
1.10.1934	..	43,083	13,906	34,891	39,204	1,589,514
1.10.1935	..	44,146	13,970	36,027	41,307	1,497,098
1.10.1936	..	44,334	14,158	36,137	42,482	1,456,033

Remarks.

Notes in circulation represents " gross " circulation (*i.e.*, total value of notes issued by the Commissioners of Currency less notes withdrawn and destroyed) and includes balances with banks and Kacheheries.

Metalic Reserve.—This refers to the specie reserve. Small silver was taken out of the Reserve in 1916 and gold coins in November, 1920. Since then the specie reserve consists of silver rupees only.

Securities Reserve consists of Sterling securities (Home, Colonial, and Indian) and Indian Rupee securities.

Market Values (Sterling converted at current rate) are those shown in statements for September published in *Gazette* and not the value (at £1 = 13·33) on September 30 of each year, shown in Annual Financial Statements, Treasury.

Currency Profits.—The figures represent profits at the end of each preceding financial year, *e.g.*, Rs. 1,456,033 against 1.10.1936 = profits for the financial year ended September 30, 1936.

APPENDIX N.

Subsidiary Coins in Circulation (Gross) at December 31.

Year.		Small silver, *i.e.*, ·50, ·25, ·10.		Nickel ·05.		Copper ·01 and ·0½.		Total.		Per capita.
		Rs.		Rs.		Rs.		Rs.		
1924	..	10,216,211	..	659,300	..	1,189.705	..	12,065,216	..	2·51
1925	..	10,840,961	..	685,200	..	1,249,706	..	12,775,867	..	2·59
1926	..	11,713,961	..	734,900	..	1,320,305	..	13,769,166	..	2·72
1927	..	12,017,961	..	754,000	..	1,384,105	..	14,156,066	..	2·72
1928	..	11,976,461	..	769,700	..	1,433,805	..	14,179,966	..	2·65
1929	..	12,178,961	..	766,900	..	1,468,705	..	14,414,566	..	2·65
1930	..	11,417,961	..	721,300	..	1,467,305	..	13,606,566	..	2·48
1931	..	10,430,962	..	672,800	..	1,446,805	..	12,550,567	..	2·36
1932	..	9,557,961	..	656,500	..	1,430,405	..	11,644,866	..	2·16
1933	..	9,382,961	..	660,700	..	1,435,505	..	11,479,166	..	2·12
1934	..	9,714,961	..	700,200	..	1,474,005	..	11,889,166	..	2·14
1935	..	9,563,961	..	707,100	..	1,487,805	..	11,758,866	..	2·10
1936	..	9,549,961	.	730,100	..	1,508,555	..	11,788,616	..	2·09

5——J. N. 81971 (2/39)

APPENDIX O.

Dates of Issue of Subsidiary Coins.

Fifty Cents	..	1892, 1893, 1895, 1899, 1900, 1902, 1903, 1910, 1913, 1914, 1917, 1919, 1920, 1921, 1922, 1924, 1925, 1926, 1927, 1928, 1929.
Twenty-five Cents	..	1892, 1893, 1895, 1899, 1900, 1902, 1903, 1907, 1908, 1909, 1910, 1911, 1913, 1914, 1917, 1919, 1920, 1921, 1922, 1925, 1926.
Ten Cents	..	1892, 1893, 1894, 1897, 1899, 1900, 1902, 1903, 1907, 1908, 1909, 1910, 1911, 1912, 1913, 1914, 1917, 1919, 1920, 1921, 1922, 1924, 1925, 1926, 1927, 1928.
Five Cents Copper	..	1870–1889* bearing date 1870, 1890, 1891, 1892–93*.
Five Cents Nickel	..	1909, 1910, 1911, 1912, 1913, 1920, 1926.
One Cent	..	1870–1889* bearing date 1870, 1890, 1891, 1892, 1900, 1901, 1904, 1905, 1906, 1908, 1909, 1910, 1912, 1914, 1917, 1920, 1922, 1923, 1925, 1926, 1928, 1929.
Half Cent	..	1870–1889* bearing date 1870, 1890, 1891, 1895, 1898, 1901, 1904, 1905, 1906, 1908, 1909, 1912, 1914, 1917, 1926.
Quarter Cent	..	1872–89* bearing date 1870, 1890, 1898, 1902, 1904.

* Date of indent.

NOTE.—*Silver rupees* issued from the Indian Mints from 1835 bear the following dates :—

1835, 1840 (two issues), 1862, 1874, 1875, 1876, 1877, 1878, 1879, 1880, 1881, 1882, 1883, 1884, 1885, 1886, 1887, 1888, 1889, 1890, 1891, 1892, 1893, 1897, 1898, 1900, 1901, 1903, 1904, 1905, 1906, 1907, 1908, 1909, 1910, 1911, 1912, 1913, 1914, 1915, 1916, 1917, 1918, 1919, 1920, 1921, 1922. (Report of the Controller of Currency, India, 1935.)

INDEX.

(Reference to paragraphs.)

G.

I.

K.

L.

M.

N.

O.